How God Wants Us to Worship Him

OTHER BOOKS FROM VISION FORUM

Be Fruitful and Multiply

Beloved Bride

The Bible Lessons of John Quincy Adams for His Son

The Birkenhead Drill

The Boy's Guide to the Historical Adventures of G.A. Henty

Cabin on the Prairie

Cabin in the North Woods

Christian Modesty and the Public Undressing of America

Destination: Moon

The Elsie Dinsmore Series

Family Man, Family Leader

Home-Making

How God Wants Us to Worship Him

The Letters and Lessons of Teddy Roosevelt for His Sons

The Life and Campaigns of Stonewall Jackson

Little Faith

Missionary Patriarch

Mother

The New-England Primer

Of Plymouth Plantation

The Original Blue Back Speller

Poems for Patriarchs

Safely Home

Sergeant York and the Great War

The Sinking of the Titanic

Ten P's in a Pod

Thoughts for Young Men

Verses of Virtue

How God Wants Us to Worship Him

An Exposition and Defense of the Regulative Principle of Worship

By Joe Morecraft III

The Vision Forum, Inc.
San Antonio, Texas

THIRD PRINTING

Copyright © 2004 The Vision Forum, Inc.

"Where there is no vision, the people perish."

The Vision Forum, Inc.
4719 Blanco Rd., San Antonio, Texas 78212
1-800-440-0022
www.visionforum.com

ISBN: 1-929241-31-3

Typography and Cover Design by Joshua R. Goforth

Printed in the United States of America

*This book is dedicated to
my children and grandchildren
who, I pray, will worship God in spirit and truth
down through their generations*

TABLE OF CONTENTS

Publishers Introduction 1

Introduction 5

1. How Does God Want to Be Worshipped? 11

2. What Is the Regulative Principle of Worship? 53

3. The Second Commandment and the Regulative
Principle of Worship 81

4. The Great Commission and the Regulative
Principle of Worship 85

5. The Elements of Worship 89

6. Common Objections to the Regulative
Principle of Worship 99

7. Popular Innovations to Worship 117

8. Musical Instruments and the Worship of God 139

9. Did Paul Do Away with the Fourth Commandment? 147

10. What Songs Should Be Sung During Worship? 165

11. The Place of Special Music in the Worship of God........ 177

12. What about Dancing during Worship? 181

13. What Does the Bible Say about Hand Clapping? 191

14. William Cunningham on the Authority of
Apostolic Example 197

Appendix A. James Bannerman on the Limits of Church
Authority in Worship Services 201

Notes... 207

PUBLISHER'S INTRODUCTION

For some time I have been urging Christian audiences to "take the desert island challenge." The challenge goes like this: Suppose you lived on a desert island, had never had contact with modern culture, and the only thing to guide you in your decision making or in formulating your worldview was the Bible. How would you live?

The desert island challenge is really just another way to encourage people to embrace and live by a wonderful doctrine the Reformers called "the sufficiency of Scripture." This doctrine is nicely summarized by the Apostle who wrote:

> All scripture is given by inspiration of God, and is profitable for doctrine, for reproof, for correction, for instruction in righteousness: That the man of God may be perfect, thoroughly furnished unto all good works.
> (2 Timothy 3:16–17)

The belief that the Lord through Holy Scripture, which is the written manifestation of Christ, can furnish the believer with everything sufficient for his faith and the practice of that faith is what ultimately separates biblical reasoning from humanistic reasoning. Christianity places every thought and action under the Lordship of Christ as revealed in Scripture, while humanism seeks understanding by relying on man's autonomous reasoning.

The dichotomy between Christian and humanistic thinking is so vast that, as Christians, we must examine our reasoning, by taking the "desert island challenge." We must ask ourselves questions such as, "With the Bible alone to guide you, would you conclude that it was acceptable to send your children to government schools to be trained by those who do not fear the Lord, and thus have 'no knowledge' (Psalm 7)?" Or, "If all you had was the Bible, would it be normative for mothers to be the spiritual leaders of their homes?" Or even, "If all you had was the Bible to guide your path, does scripture teach you to separate children from their parents in the worship service of the local church?"

The good news is that tens of thousands of parents, yearning for deeper family relationships, are beginning to ask questions like these and to seek answers from the Bible. The result has been nothing short of a Holy Spirit created revival. This revival is evident in the growth of Christian home education, the rebirth of family worship, and the rise of biblical patriarchy.

These same questions, which lead Christians to submit their family life to *Sola Scriptura* (Scripture alone), inevitably lead them to desire to submit their corporate worship to *Sola Scriptura*. In an age when it is not uncommon to see the worship service of the local church focused on a veritable smorgasbord of innovations including "laughing in the spirit," "clowns for Jesus," or "spiritual dancing," it is important that we step back and once again examine our worship practice with Scripture alone.

When the Reformers applied the doctrine of "Sufficiency of Scripture" to their examination of worship, they articulated what became known as "The Regulative Principle of Worship." Thousands of believers broke from the Anglican and Roman Catholic Churches in a sincere effort to reform worship to meet biblical standards. There were, of course, variations among the diverse groups of Presbyterians, Baptists, Congregationalists, and Separatists, but they were unified in their effort to understand what Scripture taught. They sought a pure New Testament approach to the meeting of the church, an approach that inevitably fostered some of the strongest movements of God manifested in the sixteenth, seventeenth, and eighteenth centuries.

We have published this book because we believe that the same questions concerning worship that were asked by men as diverse as John Calvin, William Bradford, John Bunyan, and Charles Spurgeon need to be asked by you and me today. Dr. Morecraft asks the same question that these men asked: Will the Bible truly be the exclusive guide for our worship, or will we attempt to improve on God's perfect revelation through human innovation?

You need not agree with every point in this book or accept each of his applications or even subscribe to Dr. Morecraft's distinctively Presbyterian understanding of reformed theology, in order to benefit greatly from his rich insights and able defense of the historic view on the Sufficiency of Scripture as applied to worship. But you must decide by what standard you will worship God. For my part, I am thrilled to see such a thorough and courageous advocacy for the authority of Scripture.

Douglas W. Phillips

Publisher

Author's Introduction

Whenever Satan sees revival and reformation going on in the church, he tries to squelch and subvert it by using the church's friends as well as her enemies. When God sends reformation, Satan tries to stir up a counter-reformation.

Over the past thirty years we have seen a revival of the church with the rediscovery of historic, reformed, biblical Christianity that had been waning in this country since the mid-nineteenth century. This revival has affected churches from a variety of denominations. It has brought about the creation of many new congregations and even some new denominations. God has raised up more men who are expounding the old faith today than have been preaching it for generations. Just as those who resisted reformation in the past tried to discredit the faithful preachers by calling them Puritans and extremists, so today's critics label reformers "Hyper-Calvinists." They ridicule their claim of trying to be truly reformed and thoroughly reformed by the Word of God, (as opposed to the "barely reformed", or the "ostensibly reformed").

Our numbers and influence are growing throughout the United States and around the world. One evidence of the strength of the new Reformation is the furious opposition that has arisen in its wake. Through the manipulation of the pride and curiosity of men, Satan has brought a new and serious threat to the reformation of the church that, if it continues, will lead to the deformation of the church and the undoing of what the Protestant Reformation has been building for four hundred years.

The heart of reformed and biblical religion is the purity and beauty of the worship of God. Today, that purity of worship is compromised by people who in most other areas share our commitment to the reformed faith.[1] This is not a small in-house disagreement—a tempest in a teapot. A breakdown in worship or a compromise of the purity of worship is like a crack in the foundation of a building. At first the building may appear sound enough, but the crack, unless it is repaired, will eventually bring about the weakening and collapse of the whole building.[2]

The biblical and reformed doctrine of worship is being threatened today from two directions within Evangelical and reformed churches. On one side are those who want more freedom and less form in worship so that, if they had their way, our worship services would look and feel more like a contemporary charismatic service. On the other side are those who are calling for less freedom and more form in worship so that, if they had their way, our worship services would look and feel more like Anglican, Roman Catholic, or Eastern Orthodox services. Both sides are making the same error: they are rejecting, even ridiculing and misrepresenting, the God-owned, time-honored, and Bible-based regulative principle of the worship of God. That is, WE MAY ONLY WORSHIP GOD IN THE WAY HE HAS COMMANDED IN THE BIBLE, AND IF IT IS NOT COMMANDED, IT IS FORBIDDEN.

The liturgists argue that we are like the Nestorians[3], denying the incarnation in our worship services because we do not have more forms and visible symbols. The other side shows its disdain for the regulative principle and its adherents by referring to us as "chauvinists" and "sourpusses." (At least they have a sense of humor.)

Many of these new critics of the regulative principle of worship are personal friends of mine for whom I have the deepest respect and love and who are greatly superior to me in gifts, intelligence, and godliness. Because of this it grieves me to criticize them and attempt to correct them because they have distanced themselves from the Reformation in their views of worship. I dare to do so because Scripture compels me. My personal preferences are not the standard of evaluation, but the Word of God as faithfully interpreted by the Westminster Standards and four hundred years of reformed thought. The battle is not between the Westminster Standards and the Word of God; but between the tried and tested confessions and catechisms of the church and the opinions of a small group of men. The innovators must be answered for the well-being of God's flock. Truth must come before friendship but because these critics are my friends and superiors, I would ask you not to interpret anything I write here as being disrespectful or unloving to them as Christian brothers.

What has amazed me is the apparent ease with which these men have cast aside the historic regulative principle of worship set forth in the Westminster Confession of Faith (1:6 and 21:1). Is the reason they fell for the critics' assertions, speculations, and misrepresentations that they themselves had not adequately studied what the Bible teaches concerning the regulative principle of worship?

We are going to examine a subject most professed Christians have never given much thought: the proper worship of God. And yet this subject is one of the most important subjects human beings can think about because it is concerned with how we worship God. In fact, worshipping God is the most important thing we ever do. Why? First, it is important because God is worthy of all our worship. "Worthy are You our Lord and our God, to receive glory and honor and power; for You created all things, and because of Your will they existed, and were created" (Rev. 4:11). Second, this subject is important because we were created in God's image to spend our lives worshipping Him in fellowship with Him, glorifying and enjoying Him forever. Third, this a critically important subject because God saved us from our sins and restored us to His favor in order that we might worship Him in Spirit and truth all the days of our lives. In Exodus 5:1, Moses and Aaron went to Pharaoh and said to him, "Thus says the Lord, the God of Israel, 'Let My people go that they may celebrate a Feast to Me in the wilderness.'" In other words, the goal and purpose of Jehovah's redemption of Israel from slavery in Egypt was that His people might be free to worship Him according to His Word.

We will be examining why we do the things we do, and why we do not do, and should not do, other things in worship services. Why not use "prescribed written liturgies" and observe holy days in the church calendar such as Christmas and Easter? Why not have vestments and clerical garb, give altar calls, come forward and kneel to receive the Lord's Supper, cross ourselves, perform drama and skits in worship, or have choreographed dances in worship? Why not use incense, pictures of Jesus, and other visual aids such as candles and crosses? Why not genuflect and salute flags in worship? Why not have a time for greeting each other or for following the many other practices of contemporary Protestant, Roman Catholic, and Eastern Orthodox churches, that are not commanded by the Word of God?

In this study we will be attempting to answer this pivotal question: How does God want us to worship Him? Not how do we want to worship God; but how does God want to be worshipped? How we want to worship God is irrelevant because what we want may not be what God wants. In worshipping Him—our great King and dear Savior—our concern must always be to please Him, not to please ourselves or to please others. As we stand before His face and under His sovereignty in worship the question cannot be: What do we want to do in worship that will please us but rather, what does God want us to do in worship that will please Him? We are not worshipping ourselves, we are worshipping the living and true God.

The way we created human beings must frame the question is this: Since all that matters are God's desires and God's pleasure, how can we determine the way God wants us to worship Him? What does He command us to do in our times of worship in order to please Him? How can we know if the elements of our worship are acceptable to Him? Just because what we do in worship satisfies us or is meaningful to us or makes us feel close to God does not mean that it is something God wants us to do. Just because the things we do in worship seem to us to be things that God likes, or because we do them in sincerity, or because they seem to be a blessing to us does not at all mean that God is pleased with us. In fact, because self-delusion is inherent in the human condition, it is very possible that a person can feel close to God when he does certain things in worship, when in fact the very things he is doing insult God and make God angry with him.

Following our hearts in determining how God is to be worshipped is a dangerous course, for the heart is deceitful above all things and desperately wicked, who can understand it? Jesus said that it is not what goes into a man but what comes out of his heart that defiles him. In Numbers 15:39 God explicitly forbids following our own illicit desires and says that our sole responsibility is to remember and obey all the commandments of the Lord "and not follow after your own heart and your eyes." Regardless of the intensity of religious feeling or the force of intellectual argument or the popularity of the practice, in the worship and service of God we are not to devise any other way of worshipping God than what He has commanded in the Bible. Neither our hearts nor our eyes, *i.e.*, our ability to perceive, may direct us in how to worship God. Human beings, regenerate or unregenerate, have neither the right nor the competence to dictate to a sovereign God how He is to be worshipped.

Why not? Because of our creaturehood and our sinfulness we are totally unqualified to determine how God is to be worshipped or to have any say or to make any suggestions in the matter. We are simply to find out what God wants and then do it. Only God has the prerogative to determine how He is to be worshipped and served by His creatures. It is the height of arrogance, superstition, and idolatry to think that we have any right to determine how God should be worshipped. How dare the clay dictate or suggest anything to the Potter!

The question remains: How does God want to be worshipped? Where can we go to find God's reply to that question? You know the only answer: to God's all-sufficient Word, the Bible. That God-breathed book is the comprehensive and completed revelation of the will of God for us by which we can be thoroughly equipped for every good work, including the good work of worship. Everything we will ever need to know about glorifying God and worshipping Him is contained in its pages. It is such a complete, perfect, eternal, all-embracing, and all-sufficient revelation from God that it will never need amendment, correction, or supplementation. As Proverbs 30:5–6 tells us: "Every word of God is tested; He is a shield to those who take refuge in Him. Do not add to His words or He will reprove you and you will be proved a liar." The faithful Christian loves and believes every word in the Bible and seeks to bring his every thought into conformity to it. As David said in Psalm 119:128: "Therefore I esteem right all *Your* precepts concerning everything; I hate every false way."

Let us leave the opinion of man behind and seek the revelation of God's mind in the Bible to find out how God wants us to worship Him. We will approach the subject in this way: first, we will consider a handful of incidents recorded in Scripture that clarify the issue of God-honoring worship. Second, we will carefully examine God's instructions in Scripture as to what is pleasing to Him in worship and what displeases Him. Third, we will look at some of the specific details of God's commands for worship. Finally, we will attempt to answer some of the objections our brothers have brought against this time-honored, Bible-based principle of worship.

CHAPTER ONE

How Does God Want to Be Worshipped?

The story of Nadab and Abihu recorded in Leviticus 10:1–7 follows a high and joyous point in the history of Israel: the inauguration and installation of Israel's first priests. Aaron, the High Priest, and his four sons, including Nadab and Abihu, were to serve God as priests in the Tabernacle worship services. The ordination service described in Leviticus 8 and 9 is high drama.

The whole congregation of Israel gathered in front of the Tabernacle. The priests were ceremonially cleansed, invested with their priestly garments, and anointed into office. Sacrifices were made on their behalf and on behalf of Israel. Blood was sprinkled on them. Their hands were filled with the authority and duties of their office. They were consecrated to God. They ate the ordination meal and made their commitments to God. Eight days later the newly ordained Aaron and his sons made various sacrifices. And then something dramatic and awesome happened as recorded in Leviticus 9:23–24:

> Moses and Aaron went into the tent of meeting. When they came out and blessed the people the glory of the LORD appeared to all the people. Then fire came out from before the LORD and consumed the burnt offering and portions of

fat on the altar, and when all the people saw it, they shouted and fell on their faces.

So would we! Imagine the awe, the reverence, and the joy the people experienced! But, what happened next was tragic. In religious fervor, reverence, exuberance, gratitude to God, zeal for His worship, and intensity of emotion, (and maybe a little too much wine [10:9]), the newly ordained priests in their priestly garments—"Now Nadab and Abihu, the sons of Aaron, took their respective firepans, and after putting fire in them, placed incense on it and offered strange fire before the LORD, which He had not commanded them. And fire came out from the presence of the LORD and consumed them, and they died before the LORD" (10:1–2).

What did they do that was so wicked and deserving of death? Brand spanking new, squeaky-clean priests—the first ones in the history of Israel—in true devotion to God, offer sacrifices that God accepts. Try to imagine their joy at God's miraculously sending fire to consume their offering! They must have been thinking, "All right! He liked it! We passed the final exam!" They decided to extend this glorious moment a little longer, add a cherry on to the icing, a flourish at the end of their signature, and God killed them for it. Why? Generally speaking, they disregarded the Lord's commandment in Exodus 25:8–9, 40:

> "Let them construct a sanctuary for Me, that I may dwell among them. According to all that I am going to show you, as the pattern of the tabernacle and the pattern of all its furniture, just so shall you construct *it*. See that you make *them* after the pattern for them, which was shown to you on the mountain."

This command was so important that it is repeated twice in the New Testament, Acts 7:44 and Hebrews 8:4–5 and alluded to one more time in Hebrews 9:1.

The tabernacle was designed as the palace and sanctuary of Jehovah and was considered the holiest place on earth to Israel in the Old Testament. God dictated to Moses in Exodus through Deuteronomy the exact dimensions of the structure itself and the precise rituals by which He was to be worshipped. Moses was commanded not to change, omit, or supplement any divinely revealed details. He was called upon by God simply to follow the pattern. No variations. God was saying, in effect, "Build the tabernacle just like I tell you; establish the priesthood just like I tell you; establish the sacrificial system and all the rituals of the tabernacle just like I tell you. Do not add to the details, and do not take away from them. Just follow everything that I tell you." Moses was to do everything in the blueprints and not to go beyond them. The reasons should be obvious. First, the tabernacle, (and later the temple), and its ceremonial details were to have a symbolic character foreshadowing Christ and His redemptive work. Second, inventions of man in the worship of God that go beyond God's command, are forbidden by Him.

The sin of Nadab and Abihu was this: motivated by religious excitement, they tried to express their worship of God in a way not commanded by God, and God killed them for it. They did not contradict a specific statute, but that they added something to their services that God had not commanded. They did not do exactly what God had ordered for His worship. Although their motives may have been commendable, they added to the blueprints.

It is difficult, however, to determine the exact nature of their sin. Several theories have been brought forward, and dogmatism about any of them is out of place. Some scholars have suggested that they got the flame in their incense pans from a source other than the altar.[4] Others say that they offered incense at a time in the order of worship not commanded by God. Still others suggest that they went into the Holy of Holies to offer incense without divine warrant. Others theorize that young priests had an unlawful mixture of incense in their pans. One modern commentator on this text has dogmatically asserted that this unlawful mixture of incense was in fact their sin; therefore, their behavior violated Exodus 30:9, which forbids offering unauthorized or strange incense; they broke

God's specific prohibition rather than adding to His law. The problem with his dogmatism is that the biblical text before us does not say "strange incense," it says "strange fire."[5] The author could have very easily said "strange incense," but he did not. There was something about the fire that made it unauthorized. Whatever the case, Nadab and Abihu attempted to worship God in a way, time, or place not commanded by God. What is the lesson for us? Although these men may have been sincere in their offering of worship to God, it was unacceptable to God because it was not in accordance with what He had prescribed in His Word. Their sin, worthy of death in God's sight, was that they did things in worship that He had not commanded. Man is not free to add to the command of God, even on the basis of sincere feeling or even if the man is a zealous, newly-ordained priest. We must be clear as to what their sin was so that we will never be tempted to commit it. They did things in the worship of God that God had not commanded them to do. They disobeyed God by adding to that Word regarding how God is to be worshipped (Deut. 12:32). As Samuel Kellogg has written: "The essence of their sin was this, that it was will-worship in which they did not consult the revealed will of God regarding the way in which he would be served, but their own fancies and inclinations . . . (they) imagined that the fragrance of their incense and its intrinsic suitableness as a symbol of adoration and prayer was sufficient to excuse neglect of strict obedience."[6]

John Knox said this about Nadab and Abihu; "In the doing of this act and sacrifice they were consumed away with fire. Whereof it is plain, that neither the preeminence of the person that makes or sets up any religion, without the express commandment of God, nor yet the intent whereof he does the same, is accepted before God. For nothing in His religion will (God) admit without His own Word; but all that is added thereto does He abhor, and punishes the inventors and doers thereof."[7]

A modern critic of our interpretation "would have us ignore what the passage says and pretend it says something very different. Instead of 'which He commanded them not,' he wants to pretend it says, 'which He had expressly forbidden.'"[8] The text could have said, "Which He had expressly forbidden," but it does not. It says, "Which he had not commanded them."[9] To what does this phrase refer? Why did Moses express it in this way? "One cannot simply explain this phrase away by arguing [dogmatically] that the sin was strange incense, [when it says strange or unauthorized fire]. The Holy Spirit says that their sin was that they did something that was not commanded. They offered fire without divine warrant."[10]

The context of Leviticus 10:1–7 makes our point for us that the phrase in verse 1 "which He had not commanded them" does *not* mean "what He had expressly forbidden", but that it means exactly what it says. In chapters 8–9, after each section of the ordination service important phrases occur, as in 8:4 and 5, "So Moses did just as the LORD commanded him . . . This is the thing which the LORD has commanded to do." Declarations such as these occur throughout the ceremony: 8:5, 9, 17, 21, 29, 34, 36; 9:6, 7, 10, 21; and in 10:7, 13, 15, 18. Every aspect of the ordination service and of all the sacrifices and rituals had to be in strict accordance with the blueprints dictated by God to Moses. There could be no alterations, supplementations, or amendments. But Nadab and Abihu did something that God had not commanded them to do.

Leviticus 5:17 contains a phrase that will clarify the meaning of Leviticus 10:1: "Now if a person sins and does any of the things which the LORD has commanded not to be done, though he was unaware, still he is guilty and shall bear his punishment." Sinning against God by doing things that the Lord has commanded not to be done is a different thing than sinning against God by doing that which He had not commanded. In Leviticus 5:17 the sin is in doing what God has expressly forbidden in His law. Leviticus 10:1 does not say that Nadab and Abihu were punished for transgressing an express prohibition but because they were adding to the worship services by doing something for which there was no divine warrant. Therefore, we have before us three forms of sin that people commit against God in worship: (1) when they do not do what God has commanded, (2) when they do what He has expressly prohibited, and (3) when they o what He has not commanded.

Do you see the point made by our text? I earnestly pray that you do and that your children will also. The Lord disciplined Nadab and Abihu with deadly fire, not because they did something in the worship of God that contradicted God's prescriptions, but because they disobeyed God by doing something in the worship that God had not commanded. Do not miss this! Compromise of or confusion about this point will eventually destroy your worship of God although you may never be aware of it.

Why did God kill them for such an act of devotion? Was God overreacting? Was He too severe? We are not left in the dark on this matter. God answered this question in Leviticus 10:3. His reason for killing Nadab and Abihu was this: "By those who come near Me I will be treated as holy, and before all people I will be honored." God is not honored when man places his word and his opinion on par with God's word as if to improve what God had commanded. Philip Martin explains: "The intensity of God's jealousy is revealed by the intensity of the event. God in Leviticus 9:23–24 had indicated His blessing on the ceremonies of ordination and institution. The following act of Nadab and Abihu in comparison with the acts of ordination and institution was a minor and insignificant act. We would be tempted to overlook such a minute sin and surmise, 'Why ruin such a magnificent event by bringing drastic punishment on the offenders?' It is precisely in the magnificence of the event that God in His sovereign immutable will reveals to us the intense jealousy which He has for His own worship which He has already revealed by word in the Second Commandment."[11]

The 19th Century Presbyterian pastor John L. Girardeau rightly concluded in a sermon on the subject of worship that

God has always manifested a peculiar jealousy for the appointed worship of His house; and no marvel, for in the worship of the solemn assembly, religion finds its highest and most formal expression, the human heart is most immediately conscious of the divine presence, and the will of the creature brought into closest relation to that of God. The divine majesty is directly before us, the glory of it blazes in our very eyes, the place is holy ground, and an act which elsewhere might be indifferent takes on the complexion of profanity. It is to assert ourselves before God face to face. The sentences of Christ's displeasure against the invasions of His prerogative are not as summarily enforced under the New Dispensation as under the old, but their fearfulness is not diminished by the fact that their execution is suspended. The Apostle Paul, in I Corinthians 3, furnishes a picture that should enstamp itself upon the minds of every Christian teacher. He represents one who has, with doctrinal correctness, laid the true and only foundation, which is Jesus Christ, and yet has built upon it a superstructure of wood, hay and stubble. Behold him, as the ordeal of the last day tries his work of what sort it is! Every false doctrine, every unscriptural element of government, every intention of will-worship perishes one after another in the fiery circle which narrows around him [the unfaithful Christian minister or teacher]; his very vestments are swept from him by its consuming breath; and he stands naked and alone—himself saved, but the results of his life-long labor reduced to ashes in the final conflagration.[12]

In other words, God dealt with Nadab and Abihu so severely to teach us that: (1) In His church His Word is Law; it may not be added to or subtracted from. He will not share His glory with another. (2) We worship a holy God Who is jealous for His name and Who will be worshipped only as He commands. (3) Good intentions, sincerity, and religious fervor do not excuse adding to or subtracting from the Word of God regarding worship. (4) John Calvin wrote concerning this Old Testament event: "If we reflect how holy a thing God's worship is, the enormity of the punishment will by no means offend us."[13] (5) Man is not free to add to or subtract from the commands of God regarding worship. As Paul Martin concluded: "Worship is not a matter of conscience and self-expression, but it is a matter of God's revelation and He very jealously guards that worship."[14]

As we examine a second incident in the Old Testament that clarified the way God wanted to be worshipped in Numbers 20:1–13, we find leaders who failed and died as Israel continued her murmuring and complaining against God's providence. Israel grumbled in unbelief. Miriam died. Moses sinned against God and was forbidden to enter Canaan. Aaron died.

Moses' sin is particularly significant. As with Nadab and Abihu, at first glance, it could appear insignificant. He failed to trust God firmly and to honor God's Word before Israel. In providing them with water miraculously, Moses *went beyond what was commanded* of him by God. He added to the Word of God in disobedience. He later was inspired by God to say to Israel in Deuteronomy 4:2: "You shall not add to the word which I am commanding you, nor take away from it, that you may keep the commandments of the LORD your God." God told Moses simply to speak to the rock and it would bring forth water. Moses also struck it with his staff. It was dramatic but displeasing to God. Therefore, Moses was punished severely by being forbidden to enter Canaan. Why? Israel must learn to live by every word that proceeds from the mouth of God. She must learn not to add to or subtract from that all-sufficient Word.

Moses struck the rock as if the miracle of providing water depended upon human exertion and not upon the power of God alone or as if the promise of God would not have been fulfilled without the smiting. . Because the people saw Moses and Aaron stumble and act in a way unworthy of their office, God punished them sternly, so that the people would be certain that no one is above the Law of God. God removed them from their office before they had finished the work entrusted to them. They could not conduct Israel into the Promised Land nor could they enter it themselves.

Gary North made this thoughtful point about Moses hitting the rock with his staff: "Worshippers can easily be lured into substituting magic for Christian faith. We can understand how easy it is for a believer to make this illegitimate substitution when we examine the case of Moses' tapping of the rock in order to bring forth water for the Israelites. Moses tapped the rock in order to get water out of it, Exodus 17:6, and he made a false conclusion: that God rewards the man who properly manipulates the talismans or implements of ritualistic power. He concluded that a one-time historical link (point of contact) between tapping a rock and getting water out of it was in fact an ontological link between ritual precision and desired effect. He was lured into heresy. The influence of the power religion of Egypt was still strong in his thinking. He began to think in terms of ritual rather than ethics, of the precise repetition of a familiar formula rather than obedience to God's revealed Word. In short, Moses adopted magic in the place of biblical religion."[15] To simplify: magic is the belief that if one performs the correct ritual precisely, he will always get the desired effect, for such precise ritual has the power to manipulate supernatural forces.

We might be tempted to think that God overreacted and that there was nothing especially wrong with what Moses did. But God looks at sin differently than we do. He takes seriously Deuteronomy 4:2, whether we do or not. *Adding to the commands of God regarding worship is tantamount to magic and hence, such additions are to be condemned as superstition.* Adding rites and ceremonies to the worship of God and then convincing ourselves that God will bless us because we said or did these things is the same thing as faith in magic. We attempt to manipulate God to act in our behalf by doing certain rites and rituals invented under the *suggestion of Satan*, to use the words of the Westminster Confession.

A remarkable passage in Jeremiah 7:31–34 provides the third incident we will study that clarifies how God wants to be worshipped. Verse 31 says: "They have built the high places of Topheth...to burn their sons and their daughters in the fire;

which I did not command, and it did not come into My mind."[16] This passage again reminds us that God does not view sin in the same way that man does. In God's sight, worshipping Him in ways He has not commanded is at least as heinous as murdering children. William Young said, "Man would revolt at the unnatural and inhuman cruelty of the burning of the fruit of one's own body before an idol. But in God's mind this is but secondary, the essential evil being that it is worship which he did not command, neither came it into His heart."[17]

Modern critics of our view say that Jeremiah is condemning Israel for expressly transgressing specific Laws of God (condemning murder) and not for doing things not commanded by Him. They "apparently assume that if it can be shown that an express violation of God's law has occurred, then explicit statements of the regulative principle by the Holy Spirit can be ignored. The statement, 'which I did not command them' is the regulative principle. The prophet's lawsuit preaching clearly presupposes that the regulative principle is an integral part of God's Law. It presupposes that God's people are to base their worship practices only on divine revelation. It makes perfect sense for God not only to condemn explicit violations of His Law, but also to remind His people of the principle that underlies purity of worship."[18] Hence, they would be punished for murdering their children *and* for adding to the Laws of God regarding worship.

Are passages such as Jeremiah 7:31 and 19:5 simply condemning disobedience to God's express and stated laws, or do phrases like "which I did not command them," mean what they plainly say?[19] Are they there just for dramatic effect? The ancient Jews were condemned by the prophet, not simply for doing what God had expressly forbidden, but for doing something God had not commanded. Jeremiah 29:23 confirms that this is what our phrase means. In that passage he condemns the false prophets because "they have spoken words in My name falsely, which I did not command them." The false prophets are cursed by the true prophet for preaching things

God did not command them to preach. Their doctrines originated in their own depraved brains.

John Calvin said the following about Jeremiah 7:31:

> God here cuts off from men every occasion for making evasions, since he condemns by this one phrase, I have not commanded them, whatever the Jews devised. There is then no other argument needed to condemn superstitions, than that they are not commanded by God: for when men allow themselves to worship God according to their own fancies, and attend not to His commands, they pervert true religion. And if this principle was adopted by the Papists, all those fictitious modes of worship...would fall to the ground. It is indeed a horrible thing for the Papists to seek to discharge their duties toward God by performing their own superstitions. There is an immense number of them, as it is well known, and as it manifestly appears. Were they to admit this principle that we cannot worship God except by obeying His Word, they would be delivered from their deep abyss of error. The prophet's words then are very important when he says that God has commanded no such thing, and that it never came to His mind; as though He had said, that men assume too much wisdom when they devise what He never required, nay, what He never knew.[20]

Echoing Calvin's concern, we must say that today's critics of the regulative principle are unintentionally putting themselves back on a path that leads to Rome. In fact several of those Presbyterians who have embraced their views have joined either the Roman Catholic Church or the Eastern Orthodox Church.

The fourth incident that clarifies the way God wants to be worshipped is in the New Testament. It is an incident in the life of Jesus recorded in Mark 7:1–23 and Matthew 15:1–20. These texts show us that the regulative principle of Deuteronomy 12:32 is not confined to the worship in the Old Testament temple, but applies in all the ways by which, and all the times in which, we worship God.[21, 22]

Jesus is condemning the Pharisees for adding ritualistic washings to the Law of God that *occurred in the home and not in the temple.*[23] These rituals were received by a tradition that had a long and distinguished history in the Jewish church. He condemns the Pharisees for following their ancient and revered rabbinical traditions in their efforts to worship and serve the Lord, for three reasons: (1) They make worship empty and vain—"in vain do they worship Me" (Matt. 15:9). (2) They follow precepts of men traditions which were handed down, rather than the commandment of God. The incident, as Matthew records it, is introduced with a straightforward contrast between the traditions of men and the commandments of God. First the Pharisees ask Christ, "Why do your disciples break the tradition of the elders?" (Matt. 15:2). Then Jesus answers, "Why do you yourselves transgress the commandment of God for the sake of your tradition?" (Matt. 15:3). (3) The keeping of such traditions causes neglect of the commandment of God, the setting aside of the commandment of God, the invalidating of the Word of God.

A modern critic of our view argues that Jesus was not condemning all traditions in the church not commanded in the Bible, but only those human traditions that obscured or contradicted the Word of God. He argues that the comments of Jesus in Matthew 15:4–5 and Mark 7:10–12 condemning the pharisaical tradition that allowed for a person to avoid providing for his aged parents as the Law requires, shows us that Christ had in mind only those traditions that nullified or contradicted God's Law. He was not condemning human traditions that did not contradict God's Law. This critic ignores the way this incident is introduced in Matthew 15:1–2 and in Mark 7:1–2: "Then some Pharisees and scribes came to Jesus from Jerusalem and said, 'Why do Your disciples break the tradition of the elders? For they do not wash their hands when they eat bread.'" Jesus challenged the rabbinical tradition, not simply because it contradicted God's Law, but because it was an addition to it. He was condemning their turning of hand washing into a religious ritual. Jesus is showing in verses 3 through 13 why "adding human requirements to God's Word is wrong. Human requirements eventually displace God's Word. The fact that Christ gives such an example does not detract at all from verse 2 where the most innocent and apparently harmless of human traditions [hand washing] is regarded as totally inappropriate. How does washing one's hands contradict, violate or set apart God's Word? Jesus condemns the Pharisees for assuming (contrary to Scripture) that religious leaders have legislative authority in the church."[24] "When church leaders give themselves authority to invent out of their own imaginations doctrines or commandments, the eventual result is declension and even apostasy."[25]

Therefore, Jesus unequivocally condemns all doctrines, commandments, and rituals in the worship and service of God that originate with man—"You are experts at setting aside the commandment of God in order to keep your tradition" (Mark 7:9). We can no more invent new rituals than we can invent new doctrines and laws. "The Church has no authority in regulating the manner, appointing the form, or dictating the observances of worship, beside or beyond what the Scripture declares on these points, . . . the Bible containing the only directory for determining these matters, and the Church having no discretion to add to or alter what is there fixed."[26]

Jesus "refused to submit to and condemned something as apparently innocent as washing one's hands. 'Washing of the hands is a thing proper enough; one could wish it were oftener practiced; but to exalt it into a religious rite is folly and sin.' The disciples of Christ were well-trained, for they knew that any human tradition, no matter how good and innocent, must not be complied with when it is given a religious significance and status by man without divine warrant. Jesus is the champion of the regulative principle [that whatever is not commanded by God to be done in worship is forbidden because it originates with sinful man]. He rejects the most innocuous of religious traditions and also shows how human traditions and laws drive out and thus set aside what God has commanded."[27]

Jesus utterly rejected human tradition in the worship and service of God because it introduced a serious deviation from the perfection of God's Law and disparaged the honor of Him whose prerogative it is to be the only lawgiver of His Church. He freed His disciples from the bondage of arbitrary human additions to the worship of God, "delivering their consciences from subjection to anything in the worship of God but His own authority"[28]

Jesus did not practice or approve, any man-made observances of worship. He is the Head, Lord, and only Lawgiver of His Church, who came from the bosom of the Father to make the supreme and final revelation of the mind and will of God. He has determined and appointed in that revelation the manner in which God wants to be worshipped, which he intended to continue unchanged and unaugmented to the end of the world.

When Jesus left this world in His Ascension, He had delivered His disciples from the yoke of Mosaic ceremonies and from being entangled in their consciences by any inventions of men imposed on them in the worship of God. He gave them all the directions and rules they would ever need for maintaining their freedom from man in the worship of God. In His sovereignty He has taken the full responsibility for instituting ordinances in His Church, for calling the persons who would administer them, and for equipping those persons with the gifts of the Holy Spirit to make those ordinances and ministries effective in edifying His sheep.

He promised His own presence with us to the end of the world in our worship and service of Him. And in all these abundant provisions for His Church He left out nothing we would ever need! It should also be noted that all those innovations to worship so popular today—altar calls, prescribed liturgies, crossing one's self, and any other such rituals were excluded by Christ. Neither He nor any of His apostles, left His Church with a prescribed form of liturgy. Therefore, anyone who imposes these additions upon His Church, does so in contradiction to Christ's mind and His whole design for perpetuating His institutions.

What were the reasons behind Jesus' condemnation of man-made traditions? (1) Man's word is not on par with God's Word, and therefore it must not be added to the commands of God regarding His worship and service. (2) Man-made traditions are not from God; they are from fallen man and for that reason rejected by God. As Jesus said in Matthew 15:13, "Every plant which My heavenly Father did not plant shall be uprooted." (3) Man-made traditions subvert and supplant God's Word. "Human additions to the ethics, worship, doctrine or church government set forth in the Bible invariably drive out what God has warranted in favor of the man-made traditions."[29]

A member of our church, in illustration of these principles told me, after my second sermon on the regulative principle, that when he was a boy, his Lutheran church had a cross in front of the sanctuary; when he returned recently after many years' absence, the empty cross had been replaced with a crucifix. The point is that once innovations begin, they increase and worsen as time goes by. (4) Man's heart is evil. "There is nothing outside the man which can defile him if it goes into him; but the things which proceed out of the man are what defile the man. That which proceeds out of the man, that is what defiles the man. For from within, out of the heart of men, proceed the evil thoughts and fornications, thefts, murders, adulteries, deeds of coveting and wickedness, as well as deceit, sensuality, envy, slander, pride and foolishness. All these evil things proceed from within and defile the man" (Mark 7:15, 20–23). "The regulative principle may therefore be seen, in a particular sense, as a natural inference from the doctrine of total depravity. The two are tied together. For example, in Exodus 20:25: 'And if you make an altar of stone for Me, you shall not build it of cut stones, for if you wield your tool upon it, you will profane it. Any work of man's own hands, that he presumes to offer to God in worship, is defiled by sin and for that reason wholly unacceptable.'"[30],[31]

Make sure you understand the point Jesus is making here: He is not condemning the traditions of the Pharisees because they are contrary to God's Word, or because they are wicked in themselves, or because the Pharisees considered them the heart and soul of true religion, but He condemns and rejects them because they originated with man and were not commanded by God. In God's worship we are to do only what God has commanded in His Word. Jesus could not have made it any clearer. As John Knox thundered, "All worshipping, honoring or service invented by the brain of man in the religion of God, without His own express commandment, is idolatry" (*Works*, Vol. III, p. 34). Jesus condemned the Pharisees for the subversion of true worship and their supplanting the Bible with their own innovative traditions and worship practices. Jesus said to them, because they were adding the traditions of the elders, "In vain do they worship Me, teaching as doctrines the precepts of men" (7:3). "Neglecting the commandment of God, you hold to the tradition of men. You nicely set aside the commandment of God in order to keep your tradition. Thus you invalidate the word of God by your traditions" (7:7–9, 13). Jesus' words are as true today as they were when He first spoke them.

Do you have the same attitude that Jesus had toward human traditions in worship not commanded by God? Or are you able to take or leave them—saluting "Christian" flags, using pictures of Jesus, and allowing Masonic rituals in worship, drama and skits? Do you consider criticism of these things unnecessarily picky? That casual attitude is far from that of Jesus, as Mark 7 and Matthew 15 reveal. His condemnation is severe and total regarding all human inventions and traditions; He knows they all amount to the worship of man, not of God, regardless of the profession or sincerity of the worshiper.

The fifth incident recorded in the Bible that clarifies the way God wants to be worshipped is also taken from the life of Jesus in John 4:1–30. In this text Jesus leads a Samaritan woman at a well to believe in Him as her Savior from sin. In the midst of His conversation with her, He makes this statement: "Woman, believe Me, an hour is coming when neither in this mountain, nor in Jerusalem, shall you worship the Father. You worship that which you do not know; we worship that which we know; for salvation is from the Jews. But an hour is coming, and now is, when the true worshippers shall worship the Father in spirit and truth; for such people the Father seeks to be His worshippers. God is Spirit; and those who worship Him must worship in spirit and truth" (John 4:21–24).

We can learn many truths about how God wants to be worshipped from these words of Jesus. First, in both administrations, Old Testament and New, worship is regulated by the same principle: "an hour is coming, and now is, when the true worshippers shall worship the Father in spirit and truth" (vv. 21-23). Jesus is not giving her a new principle; He is stating concisely what had always been true, what was still in effect while they were speaking, and what would always be true. And that principle is this: "God is to be worshipped in spirit and truth, not because the temple represents the gospel, but because of God's nature and character."[32]

This truth refutes one critic of the regulative principle, who alleges that the tabernacle/temple of the Old Testament was strictly regulated by Deuteronomy 12:32, but that worship elsewhere, as in homes and synagogues, was not. In verse 21, Jesus refers to temple worship in Jerusalem. "Therefore, when He says that the same worship principle of 'spirit and truth' that is now operative in the Old Covenant era will also be operative in the New Covenant era, He is connecting the strict worship principle that regulated the temple to the New Covenant synagogues. Thus, the idea that the regulative principle only applied to the tabernacle/temple worship is unscriptural. It is a clever attempt at circumventing the clear teaching of Scripture in order to cling to human tradition."[33]

Second, Jesus taught the woman at the well that the foundation of all worship is the revealed truth that God is Spirit. He is the living, personal, infinite God, Who speaks, acts, plans, and loves, Who possesses self-consciousness and self-determination. Being uncreated, immaterial, and nonphysical, He does not have a body like human beings. He is a living, intelligent, invisible, active, tri-personal God, without a created form of any kind. God is His perfections. As Spirit, He is infinite, immense, and omnipresent. His character and will are known only by divine revelation, so that worshipping God in spirit and truth, i.e., according to the character and will of God, is worshipping according to His revealed Word. It cannot be otherwise, for neither reason nor experience can find God unaided by divine revelation.

"Our Savior, in His interview with the woman of Samaria, makes the spirituality of God determine the nature and the kind of worship which we are to render to the Father of our spirits. But the argument goes much further—it determines the ground of the possibility of worship. There could be no true worshippers at all, there would be nothing to which worship could be consistently adapted, if God were not Spirit."[34]

This means that Christianity is a religion of the ear and is concerned with hearing, believing, and obeying God's voice rather than trying to visualize Him who is invisible (Deut. 4:12). "To worship the true God by an image is, then, the very thing forbidden [by the second commandment], because such representation is necessarily false."[35]

Third, Jesus taught her that all our worship of God must be done in spirit and truth, that is, it must be consistent with His character (in spirit) and will (in truth) as set forth in His self-revelation in the Bible. Jesus identifies truth as His Word in John 17:17, "Sanctify them in the truth; Your Word is truth." "If worship must be consonant with the nature of God, it must be in accord with what God has revealed Himself to be and regulated as to content and mode by the revelation God has given in Holy Scripture."[36]

If God is to be worshipped at all, He must be worshipped in spirit and truth (John 4:24). "Must" is *dei* in Greek, and it denotes the element of necessity in ethical and religious obligation backed by Divinely revealed statutes. It is not only all men's *duty* to worship God in spirit and truth, it is the *only way* man may worship God. This "must" expresses "a necessity that is due to God's own nature and that has always held and always will hold true."[37]

> Michael Bushell in The Songs of Zion rightly observes, "The Spirit that is the source of eternal life must also be the source of true worship. If we assume that the Spirit works only in and through His Word, it is a fair inference from this principle that all true worship must be founded upon the Holy Scriptures . . . Acceptable worship must be consonant with the character of God as it is revealed to us in the Scriptures, and must be in conformity with that sufficient rule at every point. Only that worship that proceeds ultimately from the Spirit through His Word is pleasing to God."[38]

Therefore, everything done in the worship of God must be consistent with the revealed character of God and in strict accordance to His revealed will. Nothing else may be done in the worship of God. Whatever is not worship in spirit and truth is not worship at all.

Fourth, after telling the woman at the well that all worship of God must continue to be in spirit and truth, Jesus made this statement: "For such people the Father seeks to be His worshippers" (4:23). What God seeks, He finds. He seeks such worshippers effectively because He created what He finds in them, for they cannot produce it themselves (Ephesians 2:10). What God pleases, He does (Psalm 135:6); what He desires, happens (Isaiah 14:24). The point is that what man wants in worship is irrelevant. What God desires and Who God is, is everything. In other words, the regulative principle of the worship of God is God's own desires. The only way to worship Him truly is to do so according to His desire and in the manner He commands. . It must be in accord with His revealed character and His revealed will for us, and therefore, in complete submission to the commands of His biblical revelation, without adding to or subtracting from the commands in that word (Deuteronomy 12:32). In our worship of the one true God we must do only what He has commanded us to do in the Bible, no more and no less.

Milliken wrote in the biblical Doctrine of Worship that

"The only way to truly worship the true God is to do so according to His desire. This is a reassertion of the ancient regulative principle of worship. It is God's desire, not man's, that is to regulate our worship; to abandon that is to abandon God and to begin to slip unwittingly into idolatry. Thus the nature of true worship is determined by the desire of the true God. Or to turn it around and say it another way: if we wish to worship the true God we must do it according to His revealed desire. And that desire, stated in personal terms, is for true (genuine) worshippers. It is for people who will in any place call truly upon Him: that is what matters. Even when it was tied to a specific place this was true. Now, without geographical restrictions, it is still true. The genuine God wants genuine worshippers. And that means, people who will worship Him in the manner He desires. So, the worship of true worshippers, (as opposed to false), is of a certain nature. Not now geographically limited at all, its nature is still determined by God. Jesus' way of putting it is that it must be in spirit and truth. People who worship Him in spirit and truth is what He wants—regardless of where they do it."[39]

A sixth passage that should be examined to clarify how God wants to be worshipped is not an historical incident, but an apostolic instruction recorded in Colossians 2:20–23.[40]

If you have died with Christ to the elementary principles of the world, why, as if you were living in the world, do you submit yourself to decrees, such as, "Do not handle, do not taste, do not touch!" (which all refer to things destined to perish with the using)—in accordance with the commandments and teaching of men? These are matters which have, to be sure, the appearance of wisdom in self-made religion and self-abasement and severe treatment of the body, but are of no value against fleshly indulgence.

To protect the church from those who wanted to prostitute Christianity by blending it with the philosophies, religious practices, and traditions of men, Paul wrote the book of Colossians. His answer to those who wanted to synthesize or supplement Christianity with the opinions of men is simply this: Christians are complete in Christ! All the direction and power we need for understanding God and His will, life, ethics, worship, salvation, and living for God's glory, we have in the revelation of Christ, and we do not need to go beyond Him to the opinions, traditions, and practices of man. "He who did not spare His own Son, but delivered Him up for us all, how will He not also with Him freely give us all things" (Romans 8:32).

In Colossians Paul makes his point by teaching us how unique, extraordinary, and superior the Lord Jesus Christ really is. (1). We have complete salvation from sin in His kingdom (1:13–15). (2) He is God in human flesh (1:15). (3) He is the Lord, Possessor and Creator of the universe that exists for His glory (1:15–17). (4) As the Head of the church, He not only gives to His body all the strength and direction it needs, He also is reconciling everything to Himself, since all the fullness of God dwells in Him bodily and since He has made peace with God in our behalf by His blood (1:18–22). (5) The hidden mystery of the ages revealed in the gospel is Christ in you, the hope of glory, which gives us power, motivation, and illumination (1:25–27). (6) In Christ is deposited all the treasures of wisdom and knowledge (2:1–3). (7) In Him all the fullness of Deity dwells in bodily form, and in Him you have been made complete, and He is the head over all rule and authority (2:9–10). (8) Christ is all and in all (3:8–11). In other words, He so dominates the whole creation that persons and things have significance, not so much in their relation to each other, as in their relation to Him; and by His Spirit He indwells the members of His body.

Because Jesus Christ is who He is, we, who have received Him as our Lord and Savior, are complete in Him. In His Word we have sufficient knowledge of His will for our lives (1:9–12, 28–29). We need nothing outside of Christ and His revelation for our worldviews and ethics (2:1–4, 6–7. Everything we need— for salvation, resisting sin, living for the glory of God, possessing a true view of life and the world, knowing the difference between good and evil, and for the worship of God— we have in Him. We do not need to go beyond Christ for anything in addition to what He has provided us in Himself in any of these areas. Once this is firmly grasped, we cannot be seduced, enslaved, and defrauded by false teachers.

1. We need not go beyond Him and His redemptive work for salvation from sin. We are to receive by faith alone what He has accomplished for us with no additions or subtractions, because His atonement was perfect, once for all securing eternal redemption for all those for whom He died when He died (Heb. 9:12).

2. We need not go beyond His Holy Spirit for the power and motivation to live godly and loving lives as those being renewed into the image of God by Him. We certainly do not want to subtract from His regenerating and sanctifying work within us, and we most certainly can do nothing to add to it. We can only work out with fear and trembling what He works in us: the desire and ability to live for God's pleasure.

3. We need not go beyond His written revelation for our worldview and philosophy of life. "The whole counsel of God concerning all things necessary for His own glory, man's salvation, faith and life, is either expressly set down in Scripture, or by good and necessary consequence may be deduced from Scripture, unto which nothing at any time is to be added, whether by new revelations of the Spirit, or traditions of men" (*Westminster Confession of Faith*, I, VI).

4. We need not go beyond the written revelation of Christ regarding how we should worship Him. Everything we need to know as to how we are to worship God is contained in the pages of His Word, and His directions for our worship of Him are complete. They need no additions or subtractions.

In applying the main point of the epistle to the lives of the Colossian Christians, the apostle Paul warns them, and us, against being seduced, enslaved, and defrauded by any and every philosophy or worldview that originates with the wisdom of man and not with the all-sufficient Word of Christ. I say this in order that no one may delude you with persuasive argument. "See to it that no one takes you captive through philosophy and empty deception, according to the tradition of men, according to the elementary principles of the world, rather than according to Christ. Let no one keep defrauding you of your prize" (Col. 2:8, 18).

"The elementary principles of the world" refers to all those rules and principles by which fallen and unregenerate man seeks to understand life, live in this world, and relate to God—all of which originate with man not with God. When we allow ourselves to be seduced into submitting to false teachers who act as our judge(s) (Col. 2:16), and to the empty deception of their man-made traditions and elementary principles, we are making them the lords of our consciences and are letting them take us captive to their wills. They defraud us of the riches of wisdom and knowledge that are in Christ.[41] When we submit to man as our source of truth and standard of ethics, we dilute the complete wisdom, knowledge, and power we have in Christ. We become slaves to man. "Do you not know that when you present yourselves to someone as slaves for obedience, you are slaves of the one whom you obey, either of sin resulting in death, or of obedience resulting in righteousness?" (Rom. 6:16).

We will always be seduced, enslaved, and defrauded by these false teachers when we are not holding firmly to our Head, to each other in the body of Christ, and to the means of grace by which the body grows and is kept healthy. "Not holding fast to the Head, from whom the entire body, being supplied and held together by the joints and ligaments, grows with a growth which is from God" (Col. 2:19).

Returning to man-made philosophies, religious practices, worldviews, and ethics after knowing the liberating gospel of the all-sufficient Christ is nothing less than a return to slavery to sin, Satan, and this present world system of evil around us. It is a return to thinking the way unbelievers think, confident that they are competent to determine good and evil for themselves. Non-Christians believe that their reason and experience are the source and standard of truth and religion, in worship and ethics. Therefore, we must not go back into the world and think as the unbeliever does , but we must bring all our thoughts into captivity to Christ, for in Him is all the wisdom, knowledge, and power we will ever need in order to know His will for life and worship.

Who are these false philosophers and false teachers about whom Paul warns the Colossians? They are men who offer a synthetic worldview, a blend of viewpoints: a little bit of Christianity, a little bit of the Old Testament (wrongly interpreted), some legalistic Jewish ceremonialism (2:16), some angelolatry, (2:18), and a lot of asceticism (2:20–23). This last belief involves a rigid program of austerity involving isolation from normal human society and suppression of natural physical appetites. An ascetic typically becomes almost a recluse, devoting himself completely to ceremonies of worship for the purpose of sanctification and mortification of sin, in order to become more holy, more heavenly minded, closer to God, less sinful, and more detached from this material, physical world. [42]

After giving us this warning about the false teachers, God, through Paul, explains to us the way to resist this seduction, enslavement, and defrauding in two major points:

1. Remember what you are in Christ; and think and live consistently with what you are in Him—"If you have died with Christ to the elementary principles of the world, why, as if you were living in the world, do you submit yourself to decrees, such as, 'Do not handle, do not taste, do not touch!'" (2:20–21)

2. Remember that all man-made religions and worldviews are total failures—"Let no one keep defrauding you of your prize by delighting in self-abasement and the worship of angels, taking his stand on visions he has seen, inflated without cause in his fleshly mind. These are matters which have, to be sure, the appearance of wisdom in self-made

religion and self-abasement and severe treatment of the body, but are of no value against fleshly indulgence" (2:18, 23).

The question now arises: what is our position in Christ? And Paul answers in 1:25–28, "Of this church I was made a minister according to the stewardship from God bestowed on me for your benefit, that I might fully carry out the preaching of the word of God, that is the mystery which has been hidden from the past ages and generations; but has now been manifested to His saints, to whom God willed to make known what is the riches of the glory of this mystery among the Gentiles, which is Christ in you, the hope of glory. We proclaim Him, admonishing every man and teaching every man with all wisdom, that we present every man complete in Christ." Christ is *in us* and we are *in Christ*. We are in vital union and communion with Him so that we experience the consequences of whatever He did. Because of this union, we were "buried with [Christ] in baptism, in which you were also raised up with Him through faith in the working of God, who raised Him from the dead" (2:12–13). We "were dead in [our] transgressions . . . God made [us] alive together with Him" (2:13). Therefore, we are dead to the condemning claims of the Law of God against us—"having canceled out the certificate of debt consisting of decrees against us, which was hostile to us; and He has taken it out of the way, having nailed it to the cross" (2:14); and our sins are forgiven—"having forgiven us all our transgressions" (2:13). We have been raised to newness of life under Christ's lordship and in the power of the Holy Spirit, so that now we are dead to the dominion of sin and Satan. "When He had disarmed the rulers and authorities, He made a public display of them, having triumphed over them through Him" (2:15).

Furthermore, we are now dead to the power and dictates of man-made religions and worldviews. "If you have died with Christ to the elementary principles of the world, why, as if you were living in the world, do you submit yourself to decrees . . . in accordance with the commandments and teachings of men"

(2:20–22). Therefore, our consciences feel no pain or guilt in the repudiation of man-made traditions, the elementary principles of the world, the ceremonies, holy days, and religious practices that originate with man. And we feel no pain in the exposure of their empty deceptions and their fraudulent claims.

Knowing what we are in Christ, we must live consistently with what we are in Him. When we allow ourselves to slip back into feeling conscience-bound to the elementary principles of this world rather than following consistently and courageously the sheer Word of Christ, we are relapsing, inexcusably and sinfully, into captivity to the world. We are denying what Christ has made us. We are compromising our new life under His lordship and the liberty for which Christ set us free. We are saying that we are not complete in Christ; that there must be something more, some contribution man in his pretended autonomy can make to complete our power, wisdom, and knowledge in Christ. We are saying that Christ has not made sufficient provision for us in ethics and worship; that we need the augmentation of man.

Our *Westminster Confession of Faith*, XX, II, makes a biblical statement that is one of the most liberating sentences on record. It sounds so radical and confusing to people accustomed to being slaves to man. "God alone is the Lord of the conscience, and hath left it free from the doctrines and commandments of men which are in any thing contrary to His Word, or beside it, in matters of faith and worship."

God is the only Lord of the conscience because He made it, cleansed it of evil works by the blood of Jesus, and governs it by His Spirit and Word. Therefore, only God has the prerogative to dictate to the conscience what it must feel duty-bound to perform in His strength. The conscience is free from any feeling of being duty-bound to obey *the doctrines and commandments of men that are in any way contrary to His Word, or beside it, in matters of faith and worship*. This is the very point Paul is making in Colossians 2. Our conscience, in all matters of faith, doctrine, ethics, worldview, and worship, is subject only to the authority of God in Christ and therefore, is *entirely free* from all conscience-bound subjection to the traditions and commandments of men, no matter how much pressure they use to impose them on us.

In fact, to believe any doctrine or obey any tradition in faith, ethics, and worship that is contrary to or besides the Word of God out of sense of duty is to betray true liberty of conscience. No person on earth has the authority to dictate to our conscience whom we must feel duty-bound to obey without question and without hesitation. This would be to allow that person to usurp a prerogative over us that belongs only to God, for there is only one Lawgiver, who is able to save and to destroy.[43]

All of this is particularly true of the Christian's worship of God. As James Bannerman has said: "The introduction of human rites and ceremonies into the worship of the Church, by ecclesiastical authority, very directly goes to oppress the consciences and abridge the spiritual freedom of Christ's people. In so far as the provisions of public worship are appointed by Christ, and expressly regulated in His Word, the plea of conscience cannot lawfully come in to resist their observance, or to object against the enforcement of them. Conscience has no right, and can possess no liberties, in opposition to the ordinances of Him who is the Lord of the conscience.

"Every part of Church worship, because an ordinance of God, is binding upon the conscience by His authority; it imposes a kind of obligation which no other solemnity can impose. And when, as part of that ordinance, there is introduced some rite or ceremony or appointment of man, claiming to have an equal authority, and to lay upon the conscience the same obligation, however harmless it may be in itself, it is an offense against the liberty and rights of the Christian people of the Church.

"To lay down a formula of Church worship of her own, to appoint rites and ceremonies of her own, and to enforce these under the alternative of forfeiture of Church fellowship, is a violent and unlawful encroachment upon the conscience and the liberties of Christ's people. The restriction thus put upon the exercise of Church power in public worship, by a due regard to the liberties of Christ's people, effectually excludes the introduction into it of human arrangements or ecclesiastical ordinances."[44]

We know James Bannerman was not exaggerating when, for example, we see churches accustomed to altar calls that think those who do not give altar calls cannot really believe in evangelism; or those churches that believe public worship must be according to a written, prescribed liturgy, look upon churches that follow the regulative principle as less than biblical and "baptistic."

Let me use the words of the Bible to repeat a vital principle in living the Christian life without being enslaved or defrauded by man. "It was for freedom that Christ set us free, [we must] keep standing firm and not be subject again to a yoke of slavery" (Gal. 5:1). We are conscience-bound and free in Christ to obey whatever God commands us and to avoid whatever He forbids. We must never allow ourselves to be seduced into being conscience-bound to obey man-made rules with reference to our ethics or worship of God.

This issue of liberty is fundamental and precious to those whom Christ has freed from "the guilt of sin, the condemning wrath of God . . . bondage to Satan and dominion of sin . . . from the sting of death . . . and everlasting damnation . . . (including freedom from O.T. ceremonies) . . . and from the doctrines and commandments of men, which are in anything contrary to His Word; or beside it, if matters of faith or worship. So that, to believe such doctrines or to obey such commands out of conscience is to betray true liberty of conscience" (*Westminster Confession of Faith*, XX, I–II).

To impose prescribed liturgy or any other human invention on the congregation in the worship of God is to assault and abridge that liberty for which Christ has set us free. Such impositions and innovations amount to the tyranny of man over the church of God. Much blood has been shed in the church because of the efforts of man to tyrannize the church with his inventions. Remember Henry VIII, Bloody Mary, Elizabeth I, Charles I and II, James I and II, Charles V, *ad nauseam*? From 1660 to 1688 in Scotland, over 18,000 Presbyterian men, women and children—whole families and congregations—were brutally tortured and murdered at the hands of the bloody Stuart kings for one reason: they would not submit to the king's liturgies and inventions in their worship services. They would not give up the regulative principle of worship! For them the choice was: live and worship free from the tyranny of men or die. How easy today it has been for men who have claimed to follow that great tradition to succumb to the very principles and practices for which their fathers were martyred and to succumb to those principles on such sloppy exegesis.

God calls us to stand firm, uncompromising and unyielding, for that freedom Christ died to give us and never again to subject ourselves to a yoke of slavery to man and his innovations in theology and ethics or to his impositions in the worship and service of our Lord and Savior. We must pray that God would give us a strong sense of duty to stand vigilantly in defense of that liberty and to steadfastly refuse to submit our liberated consciences to the tyranny of men. Christ shed His precious blood to set us free from the tyranny of man in the worship of God. Are you willing to live and die in defense of this revealed truth, or are you willing to accommodate yourself to additions to worship in order to keep up with the trends of the time, rather than stand against the tide? If the world and church today turn against the Bible's regulative principle of worship, are you willing to stand against the world and the church?

All abridgements of the liberty of conscience in the disciples of Christ by the imposition on them of things which He has not commanded are usurpations upon the consciences of the disciples of Christ, destructive of the liberty which He has purchased for them, "and which, if it is our duty to walk according to this gospel rule, is sinful to submit to."[45] As history teaches us over and over again, tyranny in the church leads to tyranny in the state as God's punishment upon those who allow tyranny in the church.

Second, in order to resist being seduced, enslaved, and defrauded by false teachers, we must remember that all man-made religions and philosophies are total failures. "Why . . . do you submit yourself to decrees, such as, 'Do not handle, do not taste, do not touch!' (which all refer to things destined to perish with use)—in accordance with the commandments and teachings of men? These are matters which have, to be sure, the appearance of wisdom in self-made religion and self-abasement and severe treatment of the body, but are of no value against fleshly indulgence" (Col. 2:20–23).

Paul labels these human traditions inserted in the worship and service of God for what they really are: self-made religion (NASV) and will-worship (KJV). This Greek word, *ethelothreskeia*, means self-chosen worship or self-imposed ritual—a form of worship that man devises for himself. It refers to those things people do in the worship of God that originate with man, not commanded by God, hence self-made religion. It is also translated will-worship because all forms and practices of worship that man devises for himself are not the worship of God. Rather they are the worship of the human will from which they were born. Self-made worship springs "out of man's own ingenuity—unauthorized devotion...The worship referred to is unsolicited and unaccepted. It is superstition."[46]

Paul twice makes the point that these self-made religious practices are all total failures. In 2:8, he tells us that self-made worldviews are empty deceptions; and in 2:22, he tells us that self-made religious rituals are of no value in man's struggle with sin. Since these prohibitions—do not handle, taste, or touch—do not originate in the command of God, rather than making the person who practices them a better Christian, have the reverse effect. As 2:18 says: "Let no one keep defrauding you of your prize by delighting in self-abasement and the worship of angels, taking his stand on visions he has seen, inflated without cause by his fleshly mind." How do these man-made inventions cause this reverse effect?

1. They cause him to be inflated without cause by his fleshly mind as they defraud him by deflating him of spiritual power, wisdom, and knowledge.

2. Those committed to will-worship delight in self-abasement that leads them to delight in the sense of humility they experience in self-abasement, austerity of life, and the denial of earthly pleasures.

3. They delight in "the worship of angels," for which they apparently feel the need as intermediaries to complete the mediation of Christ. They do so because they do not believe or fail to understand that the Christian is complete in Christ, in whom all the fullness of Deity dwells in bodily form.

4. They delight in taking their stand on visions they have seen. This probably refers to pseudo-visions much like their pseudo-humility. They delight in a hollow caricature of the real thing. They try to make their own ideas and practices sound as if they are on par with divine revelation, maybe even convincing themselves.

Herbert Carson says of this person described in Colossians 2:18, whose ego is inflated as he submits to human traditions in the worship of God: "Far from being humble, he is inflated with pride, for a religion which stems from man's speculation rather than God's revelation inevitably leads to self-esteem rather than humility. Yet this attitude of pride is utterly without justification for the supposed knowledge on which it rests is not true knowledge, but mere human invention. The mind which manifests such conceit is not controlled by the Spirit of God, but by the flesh."[47] For example, when a minister invents practices in worship for his congregation and sees his congregation enjoying them, he feels proud of his inventions and hopes that he will always be remembered for inventing them, thus inflating his pride while appearing humble, perhaps even to himself.

In other words, man-made practices in worship completely fail to accomplish what they claim to achieve, God's blessing bestowed on the worshipper. They may make the person who practices them feel blessed and close to God, but that does not mean that he is blessed of God just because of his subjective "feelings."

Why do the traditions of man in the worship of God totally fail to make those who practice them better Christians? Paul gives us three reasons:

1. Man-made rules and restrictions on God-given physical desires and appetites have absolutely no sanctifying power on a person where the struggle with sin takes place—in the heart, soul and mind (Rom. 7–8). These are matters which have the appearance of wisdom in self-made religion, "but are of no value against fleshly indulgence" (Col. 2:23). With scorching and stinging sarcasm, Paul summarizes these regulations as: Don't handle, don't taste, don't touch. It is as if he were saying, "Why submit to a series of don'ts, as if by adding enough negatives you would ever obtain a positive, or as if victory over sin and progress in sanctification would ever be achieved by basing all your confidence in sheer avoidance."[48]

This leads us to a vitally important but much neglected truth that the Holy Spirit does not give the inventions and innovations of man in the worship of God any sanctifying power or spiritual value. And nothing has any spiritual value or good effect on the heart and soul without the empowerment of the Holy Spirit. "Unless the Lord builds the house, they labor in vain who build it" (Ps. 127:1). As Paul said, "My message and my preaching were not in persuasive words of wisdom, but in demonstration of the Spirit and of power, so that your faith should not rest in the wisdom of men, but on the power of God" (1Cor. 2:4–5).

Without the work of the Holy Spirit, neither preaching nor the sacraments nor any of the ordinances of God have any spiritual effect on us. Furthermore, the Holy Spirit does not use any rituals or forms of worship invented by men to communicate truth, nor does He use them as instruments by which He conveys truth to the heart with spiritual power, nor does He use them as means of saving grace to the heart strengthening faith as He does with the Word and Sacraments and other divinely instituted ordinances. The Bible sanctifies us only because it is the Sword of the Spirit. Baptism with water is a means of grace only as the Spirit uses it to seal His Spiritual baptism to us. The Lord's Supper nourishes our faith only because it is spiritual food and spiritual drink. But the Holy Spirit does not bless the traditions of man in God's worship with saving or sanctifying power. They have no positive spiritual value at all.

> As human and not Divine ordinances, the Spirit of God does not employ them as means of grace; nor does He pour through the channel of their administration by the Church the tide of His spiritual influence. They are of man, and not of God; and therefore they carry with them no spiritual blessing from the Spirit...The only power which the Church is the instrument of dispensing through ordinances is the power of the Spirit, given not to human inventions, nor in connection with ecclesiastical and uncommanded ceremonies, but only to the ordinances and Sacraments appointed by God.[49]

To say this another way: in the worship of God everything must be done to the glory of God in the edification (i.e., the building up and strengthening) of the people of God. "Let all things be done for edification" (1 Cor. 14:26). "Seek to abound for the edification of the church" (1 Cor. 14:12). Edification is the goal of the ministry of the Word. It is the reason Christ instituted the office of minister and gives His ministers the gifts of the Spirit to preach and teach. It was for edification that the sacraments and all the other ordinances of God for the church were instituted, including whatever else belongs to the nature and mission of the church. God ordained everything pertaining to the church that the body of Christ may be edified, growing with a growth that is from God. And edification, as well as growth, is impossible without the Holy Spirit.

This principle, governing all church life, ministry, and mission, is that everything must be done to edify *the Church of Christ* by the Spirit for the glory of God. That most certainly does *not* mean that whatever the ministers, elders, or congregations, or any individual member judges to be edifying to people may be done in worship services. What some human being thinks is edifying may not be so and in fact, may have the opposite effect, tearing down single-hearted submission to the Word of God and encouraging a return to living like fallen, unregenerate man lives and attempts worship.

Human beings, because of our self-deception, personal prejudices, confused emotions, and other effects of our sinful nature, are not competent to judge what is edifying and what is not. Christ is the only competent judge. And He has determined and revealed what is edifying, thus limiting us to His prescribed ordinances commanded in His written Word. Jesus prayed for His disciples: Sanctify them in the truth because only the truth empowered by the Spirit sanctifies, and the truth is the Word of God.

Therefore, nothing is effective in edifying us and in sanctifying us and in making us better Christians except what Christ blesses with His Spirit. His blessing is inseparably connected to His commands and institutions revealed in the Bible. As God said to His people in Exodus 20:24, "You shall make an altar of earth for Me and you shall sacrifice on it your burnt offerings and your peace offerings, your sheep and your oxen; in every place where I cause My name to be remembered, I will come to you and bless you." In other words, God promises His people that in all the ordinances which He has appointed for the celebration of His name and for the performing of His worship, He will come to His people and bless them with His grace, as they faithfully go to these ordinances to be blessed by Him and to fellowship with Him. He comes and blesses His people in these divinely instituted ordinances of worship. But Christ does not bless with sanctifying grace the innovations of man in the worship of God. Therefore, regardless of how people feel, *no human invention in worship edifies*—neither crossing oneself, nor saluting the Christian flag, nor coming forward in an altar call, nor charismatic excesses—*nothing that originates with man as an element of worship edifies.* *If* someone is adamant that an innovation in worship is a means of blessing to him from God, he is deceiving himself.

2. The second reason for the total failure of man-made religious traditions is that all of these rules and restrictions requiring some sort of abstinence from physical things, e.g., wine, marital sexuality, rich food, polite company, various forms of wholesome pleasure, all refer to things destined to perish with the using (Col. 2:21–22). It is more than foolish to base one's hope for victory over sin and for complete salvation on the severe treatment of the body and the suppression of natural physical appetites. It did not work in the monasteries, and it does not work in Protestant churches. It is more than foolish because it is the suppression of God-given appetites, which is not only a refusal of God's good gifts to us, but also because our problem is not the nature of our God-created physical bodies, but the effects of sin on our hearts and souls. Our problem is not that we are human with physical bodies, but that we are sinners.

Such regulations and restrictions are not merely worthless as far as helping us sin less and live better Christian lives, they are actually harmful because they make God angry with us. As Thomas Watson said, "It is provoking God, because it reflects upon His honor, as if He were not wise enough to appoint the manner of His own worship."[50]

3. These man-made regulations are total failures because, although they do have the appearance of wisdom in self-made religion (i.e., delight in rigor in religious duties) and self-abasement and severe treatment of the body, they are of no value against fleshly indulgence. They do bear a faint resemblance to spiritual reality. Devotion to such regulations gives one the reputation of being wise and holy. They give a

show of wisdom. They make one appear thoroughly dedicated to fulfilling the duties of religion with great care and exactitude. Being unwilling to refuse unreasonable burdens of man-made religion, they give an appearance of humility and self-denial. Such people appear to be willing to deprive their body severely of the satisfaction of its normal physical desires, needs, and appetites for the sake of spiritual purity.

However, rather than helping believers in their struggles with sin, these *superstitious devices* hinder us in our Christian life and encourage pride. All of these ascetic, legalistic, platonic, and ceremonial regulations of life and worship originating in human wisdom dishonor God. Furthermore, they encourage fleshly indulgence. They produce in those who yield to them pride and self-righteousness. They think that by means of these man-made rules and rituals, they are drawing close to God and becoming stronger Christians. Instead the opposite is happening to them. Having begun with man, they end up with man, not God.

Critics of the regulative principle have tried to give Colossians 2:20–23 a narrow interpretation as they tried to do with Mark 7:1 and Matthew 15:1. They say that Paul is condemning *only* asceticism, ascetic practices and restrictions, and that he is not condemning human traditions that do not contradict specific teachings or statutes in the Bible. Their argument amounts to this: "It is wrong to make rules that forbid the eating of meats and other foods, but it is entirely acceptable to invent worship practices, holy days and rites [as long as they do not contradict express biblical statements]."[51]

Their interpretation of Colossians 2:20–23 has many serious problems and must be rejected as false. Over against the narrow interpretation of the critics is John Calvin's helpful explanation of our text.

> According to the tradition of men. He points out more
> precisely what kind of philosophy he reproves, and at the
> same time convicts it of vanity on a twofold account—
> because it is not according to Christ, but according to the
> inclinations of men; and because it consists in the elements of

the world. Observe, however, that he places Christ in opposition to the elements of the world, equally as to the tradition of men, by which he intimates, that whatever is hatched in man's brain is not in accordance with Christ, who has been appointed us by the Father as our sole Teacher; that He might retain us in the simplicity of the gospel. Now, that is corrupted by even a small portion of the leaven of human traditions. He intimates also, that all doctrines are foreign to Christ that make the worship of God, which we know to be spiritual, according to Christ's rule, to consist in the elements of the world, and also such as fetter the minds of men by such trifles and frivolities, while Christ calls us directly to Himself.[52]

What is the problem with the interpretation of Colossians 2:20–23 that limits its application to ascetic practices? The entirety of Colossians 2 indicates that Paul is condemning *all* human traditions that synthesize Christian faith, ethics, and worship, and not merely ascetic prohibitions. Asceticism and Gnosticism had apparently crept into the Colossian church, and Paul condemns both heresies. However, in his rejection of these false philosophies and ethical systems, he is rejecting *all* philosophies, ethics, and religious rituals that are based on human reason, experience, and tradition.

Paul's condemnation of philosophies, worldviews, and religions that originate with man is "universal."[53] In condemning asceticism and Gnosticism, Paul, by necessary inference, is condemning *all* philosophies and religions based upon the premise that man can acquire wisdom, knowledge, and morality by a proper use of his reason, unaided by divine revelation. All such traditions are empty of wisdom and knowledge, and those who follow them have allowed themselves to be deceived by persuasive arguments that have no substance (2:4). Such traditions are, without exception, empty deceptions (2:8), for one reason—they are according to the tradition of men, according to the elementary principles of the world, rather than according to Christ (2:8).

Therefore, by implication, *any* philosophy or ethical system or religious ritual that is according to the tradition of men is condemned by the apostle simply because it is based on those rules and principles by which fallen and unregenerate man seeks to understand life and relate to God. The only philosophy, ethical system, or religion that is true and full of wisdom and knowledge is the one that is based upon the revealed truth of Christ.

In Colossians 2:20–23, Paul uses the same "universal" language as in Colossians 2:8. Just as he condemns *any* philosophy and empty deception that is according to the tradition of men, rather than according to Christ in 2:8, so he condemns *any* religious regulation, ritual, or restriction that is in accordance with the commandments and teachings of men. In verse 20, he asks, "Why do you act as unsaved people who are still living in accordance with a pagan worldview and thus subject yourselves to human regulations?" Then, in verse 21, Paul gives specific examples of the human regulations he has in mind—Do not handle, do not taste, do not touch! And so we ask the critics: are the man-made regulations of verse 21 prohibiting handling, tasting, and touching people and things the only religious practices, human traditions, commandments, and teachings of men that are to be condemned? Of course not! "Given the universal condemnation of human philosophy and tradition that both precedes and follows verse 21, the human requirements of verse 21 must be viewed as a few examples taken from the universal category of human philosophy and tradition. There is no way that Paul's statement in verse 22— according to the commandments and doctrines of men, can be restricted to the regulations of ascetic Gnosticism any more than the condemnation of human philosophy in verse 8 can be restricted to one Greek sect. The interpretation that says that Paul forbids the addition of some human philosophies and traditions into the doctrines, ethics and worship of the church, yet permits other human traditions, violates standard, orthodox Protestant methods of interpretation. A study of both the Old and New Testaments proves beyond a shadow of a doubt that God forbids additions and subtractions to the doctrine, ethics, and worship set forth in divine revelation, (Deut. 4:2, 12:32, Prov. 30:6, Gen. 4:3–5, Lev. 10:1–2, 2 Sam. 6:3–7, 1 Chr.

15:13–15, Jer. 7:24, 31; 19:5, Isa. 29:13, Num. 15:39–40, Matt. 15:2–9, John 4:24, Rev. 2:18, 19, etc.)."[54]

The Book of Church Order of the Presbyterian Church in America (second edition) contains a clear and precise statement which is a practical application of Colossians 2:20–24 and the others biblical texts that teach the regulative principle of worship: "Christ, as King, has given to His Church officers, oracles and ordinances; and especially has He ordained therein His system of doctrine, government, discipline and worship, all of which are either expressly set down in Scripture, or by good and necessary inference may be deduced therefrom; and to which things He commands that nothing be added, that from them naught be taken away." In other words, because Jesus is the Head, in His church His Word, and His Word alone, is law. It is unlawful, therefore, to introduce into His doctrine, government, discipline, and worship revealed in the Bible, any innovations which have not been sanctioned by Christ in His Word. Since Christ is the King of the Church and Savior of the Body, only He may say how His worship and service are to be performed. He has revealed His will concerning His worship and service in the Bible. And He personally condemns all supplementation, correction, or abridgement of what is written in its pages.

CONCLUDING APPLICATIONS

1. From the Westminster Confession of Faith, chapter 21: "The acceptable way of worshipping the true God is instituted by Himself and is so limited by His own revealed will that He may not be worshipped according to the imaginations and devices of men."

2. A worship service is the province of God, not of man. The church may no more add to the ordinances and practices of worship prescribed by God in His Word than it can add to the doctrines of Christ. It is a steward and administrator of the mysteries instituted by Christ, and not the inventor or framer of new mysteries of its own.

3. God is vitally concerned about the way He is worshipped. He did not leave it to the ingenuity of man's depraved mind to devise a worship system that would be acceptable to Him.

4. Why would anyone want to add to or subtract from the command of God regarding worship? Why would anyone not be satisfied with the biblical regulative principle of worship? Why would anyone not want to do in worship only what God has commanded? Two reasons come to mind: pride and curiosity. Robert McCracken says, "Man's pride often leads to impertinence in worship."[55] John Calvin said that the reason people add to the worship of God is because they "take it for a principle that they always have some reason with them, and that they are of sufficient ability to govern themselves as they ought to do. Thus, then pride takes the first place, when men discern between good and evil after their own fancy. Contrariwise, God's will is to be wise for us, and that we as silly sheep should hearken to our Shepherd's voice, and quite forget the sufficiency which the unbelievers imagine themselves to have. Let us think there is nothing in us but error and folly, there is nothing but vanity and falsehood, until our God has taught us. That is the point that God would bring us to. But it is exceeding hard for men to restrain themselves continually from being puffed up with this fond overweening of self-wisdom, [i.e., they esteem too highly and too conceitedly their own wisdom]. And therewithal is mingled curiosity. Our ears itch to have this and that, we make discourses, we have our imaginations, and a number of things do run in our heads. Why should this not be good, we say? Why should that not be lawful? Because then that curiosity has taken so deep root in our minds, therefore God cannot hold us to the pure simplicity of His word."[56]

5. "Disobedience to God's directions for worship is sin, and brings punishment. Furthermore, sin is aggravated when we know what is right, but stubbornly follow our self-will

anyway. The sin of introducing human designs into the worship of God, contrary to what God has commanded, is much more serious to those who know what God commands and simply decide to reject it."[57]

6. In the light of what we have learned about how God wants to be worshipped from these incidents recorded in the Bible, what is our duty as Christians?

   a. The careful observance of the worship of God and the ordinances of worship commanded by God.

   b. The keeping pure and entire the worship of God and all His ordinances.

7. If reformed churches are to continue to exist in the United States, we must not only do our duty in keeping our practices in the worship of God biblical, we must also teach our children to love worshipping God according to His commands as well as detest all other forms of worship as the worship of man. Beware of those who would try to seduce you away from the pure worship of God as He has commanded us, either in the direction of more form and less freedom or of less form and more freedom. Stand firm, unbending as a stone wall and resist all change whatsoever regarding what God has commanded in His Word as to how He is to be worshipped, either by addition or subtraction. The Lord honors those who honor Him.

"The church can have no opinion and frame no laws of her own. Her whole duty lies in believing and obeying. She can create nothing. There is no necessity for it even if she could. All that she requires is already provided for her by the wisdom and mercy of her Head. She is completely equipped for all the [critical issues and decisions] of her life, and for all the ends which her Lord has designed her to achieve. The extent of her power is thus easily defined,—it consists in first knowing, and then applying the rule of faith and duty which expresses to her the will of Christ" (John L. Girardeau).[58]

Chapter Two

What is the Regulative
Principle of Worship?

How does God want us to worship Him? He answers in Deuteronomy 4:2 and 12:32:

> You shall not add to the Word which I am commanding you, nor take away from it, that you may keep the commandments of the Lord your God which I command you.

> Whatever I command you, you shall be careful to do; you shall not add to nor take away from it.

Israel is poised to enter, conquer, and occupy Canaan, the Promised Land. The leadership is about to change from Moses to Joshua. But before Moses passes off the scene, God's Spirit inspires him to give Israel the book of Deuteronomy to show them how God wants them to build a new civilization in the land. In the first three chapters, He gives them the motive and basis for their invasion of Canaan—the gospel of covenant promise and of God's mighty acts of redemption in history. Then, beginning with chapter 4 and going through chapter 27, Moses gives this redeemed people God's law for everything from worship services at the tabernacle, to marriage relationships, to agriculture and politics. And the book concludes in chapters 28 through 34 with a national renewal ceremony and the blessing and song of Moses before his death.

It is within this context that we are to understand Deuteronomy 4. In 4:1–8, we read of God's call to complete obedience to the entirety of His Law. In verses 9–31, Moses reminds God's covenant people of the nature and character of their Redeemer and Covenant Lord: He is Spirit, a consuming fire, and compassionate. Therefore, they are to worship Him in spirit and in truth. In urging Israel to obey God's Law, 4:1–8, Moses defines the nature and effects of that obedience and the purpose for which God gave His people this sovereignly dictated order of life. Their obedience must be careful, comprehensive, and perpetual. It should be without any addition to or subtraction from the Law. Obedience must be from the heart. It includes educating their children and grandchildren in that Law. The purpose of God's Law is that it is a manual and strategy for civilization building. It has an evangelistic impact on the nations. God is *near* that nation that obeys Him, so that whenever they call on Him, He answers. No ethical system on earth exists that is as just and perfect as this Law which God gave His people through Moses. God's Law is to govern every facet of His people's lives as individuals, families, and nations. We as His people are commanded to recognize no other source of truth and no other moral standard but that which is revealed in the written Word of God. And never are we to allow man to enslave us by adding to or subtracting from that all-sufficient Word.

Proverbs 30:5–6 tells us, "Every word of God is tested; He is a shield to those who take refuge in Him. Do not add to His words lest He reprove you, and you will be proved a liar." Or as God told Joshua, Moses' successor: "Only be strong and very courageous; be careful to do according to all the law which Moses My servant commanded you; do not turn from it to the right or to the left, so that you may have success wherever you go. This book of the law shall not depart from your mouth, but you shall meditate on it day and night, so that you may be careful to do according to all that is written in it, for then you will make your way prosperous, and then you will have success" (Joshua 1:7–8).

Deuteronomy 12 relates this principle of the all-sufficiency and comprehensive, final authority of the Word of God to worship. The principle of *Sola Scriptura* is here applied to the worship of God. The statutes of this chapter regulate Israel's worship of God. In 12:1–3, the command is given to destroy all temples and monuments of idolatry throughout the whole land of Canaan. Verses 4–19 contain the command to Israel to worship Jehovah at the place He chooses to reveal His name, i.e., the tabernacle. When the people gather there, they must worship God just as He has commanded them. In verse 8, we are told that no one may worship God when, where, and how he will, doing whatever is right in his own eyes. In verses 20–21, the Word of God regulates worship in the families of the land. And in verses 29–32, we see that as Israel conquers and possesses the whole land of Canaan, they are not to allow themselves to be influenced by the way the Canaanites worship and serve their gods. Rather they are to be faithful to the Word of God as the one and only regulative principle of worship. Therefore the chapter concludes with verse 32, where the Lord says: "Whatever I command you, you shall be careful to do; you shall not add to nor take away from it."

Deuteronomy 4:2 is broader in its scope than Deuteronomy 12:32 because the purpose of 4:2 is to establish the all-sufficient and all-embracing Law of God, while 12:32 is concerned with the sufficiency of God's Laws regarding worship. The Bible is such an all-sufficient rule of faith, ethics, and worship that it teaches comprehensively "what man is to believe concerning God, and what duty God requires of man" (Larger Catechism Q. 5). As long as the world lasts, it will never need any correction or supplementation by man. As our *Westminster Confession of Faith* states, "The whole counsel of God, concerning all things necessary for His own glory, man's salvation, faith and life, is either expressly set down in Scripture, or by good and necessary consequence may be deduced from Scripture: unto which nothing at any time is to be added . . ." (I, VI). Deuteronomy 12:32 specifically applies this principle to the area of worship.

All the reformed confessions emphasize the exclusive, absolute, sufficient, and final authority of the Bible as our *only* rule of faith, practice, and worship. The Belgic Confession states: "We believe that those Holy Scriptures fully contain the will of God . . . the whole manner of worship which God requires of us is written in them . . ." (Art. 7). The *Westminster Confession of Faith* states, "The acceptable way of worshipping the true God is instituted by Himself, and so limited by His own revealed will, that He may not be worshipped according to the imaginations and devices of men, or the suggestions of Satan, under any visible representation, or any other way not prescribed in the Holy Scripture" (XXI, I). "God alone is the Lord of the conscience, and hath left it free from the doctrines and commandments of men which are in anything contrary to His Word; or beside it, in matters of faith and worship. So that, to believe such doctrines, or to obey such commands, out of conscience, is to betray true liberty of conscience . . ." (XX, II). "Good works are only such as God hath commanded in His Holy Word, and not such as, without the warrant thereof, are devised by men, out of blind zeal, or upon any pretence of good intention" (XVI, I). "The whole counsel of God, concerning all things necessary for His own glory, man's salvation, faith and life, is either expressly set down in Scripture, or by good and necessary consequence may be deduced from Scripture" (I, VI). The *Westminster Shorter Catechism* describes the whole Bible as "the only rule to direct us how we may glorify and enjoy Him" (Q. 2); and the *Larger Catechism* describes it as "the only rule of faith and obedience" (Q. 3). And the *French Confession of Faith* states concerning the Bible, "And seeing this is the sum of all truth, containing whatsoever is required for the worship of God and our salvation, we hold it not lawful for men, no, for the angels themselves, to add or detract anything whatsoever to or from that Word, or to alter any whit at all in the same" (Art. 5).

In this concluding exhortation of Deuteronomy 12:32, God's people are called upon to obey with great carefulness and diligence "whatever I [God] command you." This statement, along with the similar one in Deuteronomy 4:2—"you shall keep the commandments of the LORD your God"—teaches us two important truths. First, we are to obey whatever the Lord our God commands us. God is to be obeyed, and we are duty-bound to obey Him. He does not share that lordship over us and over our consciences with any man. Whatever *God* commands us, we are to do.

Second, we are to obey *whatever* God commands – God's revealed will concerning His worship – regardless of what it is, and in all its details. We obey simply because it is God who commands these things, and as His covenant children we should need no additional reason. We are His people, bonded to Him forever, saved by His grace, claimed by Him for His own purpose, and purchased for God by the blood of Jesus. Therefore, having been bought with such a price, we are not our own, and we are to spend our lives glorifying and enjoying Him under the government of His Word in the power of His Spirit.

We are to be so careful in our obedience to God's Word concerning worship that we may neither add to nor take away from it. "Take away" refers to a lessening of God's commands, and "add to" refers to an increasing of God's commands with additional human rules and rituals placed on par with God's ordinances. Both subtraction from biblical law and additions to it detract from the majesty of God's Law and eventually subvert and supplant it with the traditions of men (Matt. 15:6; Isa. 10:1–2, 29:13; and Jer. 8:8). In other words, biblical law is so perfect and so comprehensive, being a transcript of God's character and will for us, that any alteration, supplementation, or amendment of would be an arrogant assault by sinful man on the majestic sovereignty of the triune God.

How does a person subtract from God's Law? By disobeying it, neglecting it, editing it, or treating it as obsolete and irrelevant. How does he add to it? By imposing upon the human conscience laws to live and worship by which do not originate in biblical law. John Calvin said: "Seeing God has spoken it, it is not lawful for mortal man to interlace anything with it, but they must be content with that which they have

57

heard of such a Master. And this is not said in this place only (Deut. 4:2)...the Scripture is full of it."[59]

We may no more add to the ordinances and practices of the worship of God than we may add to the plan of salvation or to the doctrines and laws of the Bible. The sovereign God is our supreme Lawgiver. "As His sovereignty extends to His worship, so it is His sole prerogative to appoint the laws of His worship, to command His subjects the way they ought to worship Him. Can it be anything other than presumption in a subject of the Absolute Sovereign to offer as worship anything which has not been commanded? Can the inventions of the human will be set on the same level as the commands of the Divine will as proper material of worship?" (William Young).[60]

The great Scottish church historian and exegete, James Bannerman, reminds us that our argument for the regulative principle is one of long-standing in the Church:

> Any worship beyond the limits of Scripture direction is an
> approach to God unwarranted and unblessed; any attempt at
> intercourse with God, except through the regulated channel
> and authorized manner of such intercourse, is presumptuous
> and unsanctioned. The worship of the Church's own
> invention or appointment is "will-worship," ethelothreskeia ,
> Colossians 2:23; the addition to God's words or God's
> ordinances being as impious and unlawful as any alteration or
> diminution. The command, Thou shall not add to them,
> when applied either to the truths or the ordinances of Christ,
> is as valid and binding as the precept, Thou shalt not take
> from them. The proper walk of the Church in both cases is
> within the boundaries of what is expressly revealed in
> Scripture, and up to those boundaries. The one grand office
> of the Church in reference to this matter is to administer and
> carry into effect the directory of worship found in the Bible .
> . . there is a sufficient directory in doctrine laid down in the
> Bible to furnish the Church with those principles of truth
> which enable it to determine controversies of faith . . . And
> so with regard to matters of worship. There is a sufficient
> directory for worship laid down in the Bible to furnish the
> Church with those principles of order which enable it to
> regulate every new case occurring in regard to the outward

worship of the Church which requires to be regulated; and it does so in this instance also, not by adding new rules or institutions to the service of the Church, but by ministerially declaring and making application of the old to the particular matter of order to be settled." [61]

When the Bible tells us not to subtract from or add to what God commands us, it is telling us to *keep pure and entire the worship of God and its ordinances.* "Whatever I command you to do, you shall be careful to do; you shall not add to [you must keep it pure] nor take away from it [you must keep it entire]." To keep the worship and ordinances of God *pure* is to keep constant vigilance and to make the utmost effort to preserve God's ordinances of worship from any and all mixture with rites and practices invented by man. In keeping the worship of God *pure* we are "to allow or practice nothing but what is warranted by the rules which God has given us in His Word in opposition to those who corrupt His worship by intruding those ordinances into it which are of their own invention." [62]

To keep them *entire* is, in faith, to practice diligently and regularly *everything* God has commanded in His worship, not leaving out the smallest detail in its season or appropriate time, walking blamelessly in *all* the commandments and requirements of the Lord (Luke 1:6). Just as our observance of God's ordinances of worship is to be entire, so our efforts to keep those ordinances pure must be with reference to the entire service of divine worship in all its details, compromising in nothing that God has commanded and allowing nothing in our worship that God has not commanded.

Before we go on to clarify and explain the fullness of the regulative principle of worship, we need to answer its critics regarding the applicability of Deuteronomy 4:2 and 12:32. Their argument is that Deuteronomy 4:2 is too broad to apply to the regulative principle, and Deuteronomy 12:32 is too narrow to apply it today.

First, they say that Deuteronomy 4:2 refers to the entirety of the Law of God and not simply to laws governing worship. It does not literally mean that we are never in any instance to do anything that God has not commanded us to do in His Law. Rather it is a general exhortation to obey the entirety of God's Law, which also allows a great deal of liberty in how we serve and worship God. One such critic argues: "Very few regulativists would seriously argue that God's intent here is to forbid Israel from doing *anything whatsoever* in *any* area of life that is not specifically commanded in the Law. I suppose those Amish who eschew buttons for want of finding them mentioned in Scripture might look somewhat favorably on this interpretation, but they'd be mighty lonely in so doing. Yet that is precisely the conclusion which cannot be evaded if 4:2 is cited as supportive of the Regulativist's reading of 12:32. Deuteronomy 4:2 is a *general rule*, requiring a life that conforms to God's disclosed will *in its entirety*. Thus 4:2 *as a parallel demonstrates that 12:32 is not to be taken in an absolute sense.*"[63]

This critic's argument is a popular one but he commits the *post hoc ergo propter hoc fallacy*: "Since all of life contains many activities that are not strictly regulated, that are left to the free choice of man (e.g., 'Should I wear blue pants or gray pants?'). Therefore, the virtually identical regulative principle proof text passages such as Deuteronomy 12:32 must also be interpreted in such a manner that leaves man a great deal of liberty in the sphere of worship."[64]

In this argument our critic fails to distinguish between divinely revealed commands in the Bible and those actions that fill up life, which are not good or evil in and of themselves, e.g., drinking wine, eating meat, wearing buttons, brushing teeth, etc. However, even these actions, ethically indifferent in themselves, are to be governed by the Word of God. (1) They must be done to the glory of God (1 Cor. 10:31). (2) We must avoid doing these things if doing them causes our brother to sin (Rom. 14:21. (3) They should not be done if they cannot be done in faith with a clear conscience (Romans 14:14, 23). (4)

They cease to be ethically indifferent when a person becomes slavishly addicted to them (1 Cor. 6:12).

Therefore, the assertion of Deuteronomy 4:2 forbidding addition to or subtraction from biblical law is to be taken in the plain sense of the words, without equivocation. Only God can expand His Word, as He has done with the sixty-one books of the Bible that follow Deuteronomy. However, man is not permitted to add to or subtract from God's commandments. He is to obey them. "In other words, God is the *sole* source of ethics for personal, family, institutional, and civil life. Men do not have ethical autonomy. They do not have any authority to make up ethical absolutes, nor are they permitted to ignore or detract from God's Law in any way…Men do not have the authority to declare a thought, word or deed evil or sinful apart from proving such by a biblical commandment or deduction from the Bible."[65]

The fact that life is full of these actions that are not good or evil in themselves does not mean that Deuteronomy 4:2 is not to be taken in a strict sense. Human beings do not have the liberty, authority, or competence to add to or subtract from any commandment God has given us to obey, especially in the area of worship. Schwertley's comments offer insight on this point:

> However, [as we shall see] men do have a great deal of liberty in areas that are circumstantial or incidental to worship itself, [e.g., the time and place of worship, with or without chairs, etc.]. [Our critic's] arguments fail to recognize the distinction between ethics and adiaphora, worship ordinances and the circumstances of worship. If opponents of the regulative principle of worship want to use Deuteronomy 4:2 as a proof text against the reformed understanding of a strictly regulated worship, they need to demonstrate that worship ordinances belong to the sphere of life that is adiaphora. Are the parts or elements of worship that are delineated in Scripture in the same category as riding a bike, or wearing blue pants instead of gray pants ? The answer is: obviously not. Adiaphora refers to matters that are indifferent to ethics (e.g., Should I boil my eggs or scramble them for breakfast?). That is, they involve activities that are neither commanded

nor forbidden, and therefore the decision whether or not to commit the act or not commit the act does not involve sin or a violation of God's Word...Worship ordinances do not involve the liberty to do as one desires and therefore cannot be placed in the category of adiaphora. Are Christians free to omit or add to the elements of religious worship as they please? Can a church lawfully eliminate the Lord's Supper and replace it with a new sacrament. Because worship ordinances are required by Scripture, they should never be treated as adiaphora. Rather, they should receive the same treatment as God's moral law. Areas of life that are adiaphora correspond not to worship ordinances but to the circumstances of worship (e.g., Should we start the service at 10:30 p.m. or 11:00 a.m.?).[66]

Second, the critics say that Deuteronomy 12:32 regulates exclusively the sacrificial and ceremonial worship of the tabernacle/temple, all of which foreshadowed the work and ministry of the Messiah, and therefore were abrogated when He, the substance or reality behind these shadows, arrived on the scene. For this reason the laws of the sanctuary were to be strictly obeyed so that no misrepresentation of the work of Christ would creep into Israel's worship. Hence, our critics argue that Deuteronomy 12:32 has no application in the New Covenant era since Christ, who was foreshadowed in these regulations, has come. Now, what are the problems with this interpretation? Many!

First of all, if this view is accepted, then one must conclude that all other worship in Israel—in their homes and synagogues—was unregulated, and the Israelites could do whatever they wanted as long as they did not violate the express statutes of the Law. One must also conclude that since the regulative principle was abrogated with the death of Christ, which made the worship services of the tabernacle/temple obsolete, "the new covenant church has nothing to do with the regulative principle and has liberty to devise rites, ceremonies and holy days as it desires, as long as the human inventions do not violate or contradict God's Word."[67] The problem with these conclusions is that they contradict Leviticus 10, Numbers

20, Jeremiah 7, Mark 7, John 4, and Colossians 2, as we have seen.

Second, the argument that since Deuteronomy 12:32 is in a section of the Mosaic legislation that deals primarily with the worship rites connected with the tabernacle, it *only* applies to the Old Testament tabernacle worship services, is simply assumed without exegetical proof by our critics. Neither Deuteronomy, nor any other text in the whole Bible, teaches us to believe that the principle of no addition or subtraction set forth in Deuteronomy 12:32 is limited to the rites of the tabernacle. Furthermore, its context proves the opposite! While Deuteronomy 12 does in fact govern tabernacle worship regarding sacrifices and offerings, the immediate context of 12:32 speaks "to the matters of the repression of idolatry and syncretism with pagan worship that can occur not only at the Tabernacle but throughout the land of Israel."[68]

> When the Lord your God cuts off before you the nations which you are going in to dispossess, and you dispossess them and dwell in their land, beware that you are not ensnared to follow them, after they are destroyed before you, and that you do not inquire after their gods, saying, "How do these nations serve their gods, that I also may do likewise?" You shall not behave thus toward the Lord your God, for every abominable act which the Lord hates they have done for their gods; for they even burn their sons and daughters in the fire to their gods. Whatever I command you, you shall be careful to do; you shall not add to nor take away from it. (Deuteronomy 12:29–32)

What does the immediate context of 12:32 tell us? That God's concern in giving this exhortation is not simply to regulate worship at the Tabernacle, but to regulate worship practices through the whole Land of Promise.

> If Deuteronomy 12:32 only applies to the central sanctuary, why would it be used as a foundational verse to suppress pagan idolatry throughout the land? Pagan Canaanite worship was decentralized with house idols, local pagan sacred sites, local high places and sacred groves. Are we supposed to believe that Deuteronomy 12:32 is only

concerned with syncretism within the Tabernacle proper? Is
verse 31 only concerned with suppressing child sacrifice
within the Tabernacle? Of course not! The context of
Deuteronomy 12:32 proves that it cannot be restricted to the
Tabernacle/Temple.[69]

Third, the argument that Deuteronomy 12:32 applies only
to the sacrificial and ceremonial worship of the tabernacle,
which, being foreshadows of Christ, were abrogated with the
coming of Christ, ignores the fact that the worship at the
tabernacle and temple included both *ceremonial* rites that
foreshadowed Christ and *non-ceremonial* ordinances of God to
be included in all worship of Him throughout the ages. The
sacrificing of the animals on the altar was a ceremonial "type"
of Christ and His work, but the reading of the Law of God,
prayer, and the singing of praise were not ceremonial. Rather
they are "all integral aspects of Christian worship *after* the
dissolution of the Temple and the abrogation of ceremonial
ordinances. Therefore, it is overly simplistic and exegetically
unsound to argue that the regulative principle was annulled
with the ceremonial order. If the regulative principle applied to
the Temple worship, then it also regulated the non-ceremonial
worship that occurred there."[70]

The critics of the regulative principle wrongly make "a *total*
antithesis between Temple worship and synagogue/Christian
public worship."[71] The temple did in fact "typify" Christ, but it
was also the central place of the worship of God (John 4:21,
Matt. 21:13). Michael Bushell correctly addressed this principle
in *The Songs of Zion*:

> To the Old Testament Jew, the Temple ritual was the very
> epitome of worship, and all exercises of piety were in one
> way or another related back to that source. Liturgical
> practices in the synagogue in many instances corresponded
> directly to those of the Temple. Prayer, for example, was
> offered in the synagogue at the time of the Temple offerings.
> Outside, the Temple prayer was always offered facing the
> Temple or Jerusalem. The synagogues were considered
> sanctuaries in miniature, even to the point that the furniture
> in the synagogue (such as the Ark and the seven-branched

candelabra) was patterned after that of the Temple. Considering, therefore, the importance of the Temple even for worship outside of Jerusalem, it would seem reasonable to postulate a greater degree of continuity between Christian worship practice and certain aspects of the Temple liturgy than most authorities are willing to admit. The paucity of references in the literature to the influence of the Temple liturgy on Christian worship is an unbalanced situation that needs very much to be corrected. It is our opinion that the Temple rather than the synagogue is the ultimate source of a number of the most important aspects of Christian worship. That many of these aspects may have been mediated by the synagogue is beside the point, at least in so far as our concern with the subject goes. [72]

Fourth, Deuteronomy 12:32 "cannot be interpreted in isolation from the virtually identical *Sola Scriptura* passages that apply not only to the tabernacle/temple but to all of life. The *Sola Scriptura* passages teach that the church does not have autonomy or legislative authority with respect to doctrine, ethics, or worship ordinances...The regulative principle is simply *Sola Scriptura* applied to the sphere of worship. Those who apply Deuteronomy 12:32 to the temple do so only because they do not understand Deuteronomy 4:2 and the full implication of *Sola Scriptura*."[73]

John Owen, the prince of the seventeenth century English Puritans, gives us a helpful explanation of Deuteronomy 12:32 and its implications. He points out that, although this verse has immediate reference to worship as it was instituted in the Old Testament, worship was instituted only as God Himself had appointed. Therefore, while God requires that all people worship Him, He has never given up the right to dictate how He is to be worshipped in the New Testament – that right which He so zealously vindicated in the Old Testament. Such texts as Deuteronomy 12:32 have as their main point that the revealed will of God is the only rule of His worship and of everything involved in that worship. God's authority is the only governing principle regarding how He is to be worshipped. Consequently, He never did, nor ever will, allow the determination of human beings to be the regulative principle of

His worship. This is also the sum and substance of the Second Commandment.

In these texts, according to John Owen, the Lord asserts His own authority and will as the final and only rule governing all worship offered to Him by His creatures. God never delegated to any human being the authority to determine how He is to be worshipped. Therefore, this assertion of God's will regarding worship should make us careful never to presume that we share prerogatives with God as if we were His equals. No instance can be found in the Bible of God accepting any innovations in worship not appointed by Him.

In order to avoid the force of Deuteronomy 12:32, it is sometimes argued that the intention of these rules and prohibitions is to prevent only those additions to worship that are contrary to what God has commanded, not those additions that improve worship. But, the truth is that whatever is added is contrary to what is commanded because the command is that nothing be added. It is not the nature of an innovation in worship that is being condemned; it is the very idea of innovation not commanded by God in His Word.[74]

Now let us move on to clarify and explain the fullness of our regulative principle of worship. It can be stated in three short sentences:

Whatever is commanded is required.

Whatever is forbidden is prohibited.

Whatever is not commanded is forbidden.

The first two sentences are obvious in their meaning. If God has required us to do something in His worship, we must do it. If God forbids us to do something in His worship, we may never do it. The third sentence is also obvious; it is the practical application of Deuteronomy 4:2 and Deuteronomy 12:32. If God has not commanded us to do something in His worship, we may not do it because God is to be worshipped only according as He has commanded. To do otherwise would add to the commandment of God which Deuteronomy 12:32 strictly forbids. Therefore, whatever is not commanded is forbidden by its very nature, for it is an attempt of man to supplement the word of God.

However, it seems that most churches today replace the third sentence with this one: Whatever is not forbidden is permitted. In other words, if God has not forbidden a certain rite or action in worship, then we may do it. Once again, this is tantamount to adding to the Law of God, which Deuteronomy 12:32 forbids. Furthermore, the principle opens a Pandora's Box of new and innovative religious practices originating in the brain of man, which as Jesus said in Mark 7, would eventually lead to the subverting, neglecting, supplanting, and invalidating of the Word of God.

The wisest and most precise explanation of the Bible's regulative principle of worship is found in the Westminster Standards.

> The whole counsel of God, concerning all things necessary for His own glory, man's salvation, faith, and life, is either expressly set down in Scripture, or by good and necessary consequence may be deduced from Scripture: unto which nothing at any time is to be added, whether by new revelations of the Spirit, or traditions of men. (Westminster Confession of Faith, I, VI)

> The acceptable way of worshipping the true God is instituted by Himself, and so limited by His own revealed will, that He may not be worshipped according to the imaginations and devices of men, or the suggestions of Satan, under any visible representation, or any other way not prescribed in the Holy Scripture. (Westminster Confession of Faith, XXI, I)

> The duties required in the second commandment are, the receiving, observing, and keeping pure and entire, all such religious worship and ordinances as God hath instituted in His Word . . . as also the disapproving, detesting, opposing, all false worship. (Westminster Larger Catechism Q. 108)

> The sins forbidden in the second commandment are, all devising, counseling, commanding, using, and any wise

approving, any religious worship not instituted by God Himself . . . all superstitious devices, corrupting the worship of God, adding to it, or taking from it, whether invented and taken up of ourselves, or received by tradition from others, though under the title of antiquity, custom, devotion, good intent, or any other pretence whatsoever. (Westminster Larger Catechism Q. 109)

Some recent critics of the regulative principle have tried to refute the historic reformed view by defining the term far narrower than have any previous adherents. Those critics have explained the sentence, "whatever is not commanded is forbidden," as meaning that, unless an explicit, divine verbal imperative can be found in the Bible for a worship practice, it is forbidden. I know of no adherent to the regulative principle of worship in the entire history of the reformed faith to hold to that narrow view. It is a man of straw.

The *Westminster Confession of Faith* makes clear that we can know whatever is necessary for glorifying God in worship by: (1) Divine commands *expressly set down in Scripture*, and (2) Divine commands that are *by good and necessary consequence deduced from Scripture*. So "that which may be derived by good and necessary consequence from the express statements of Scripture is no less binding than an express command itself. Approved example has equal validity with a direct command, and even where approved example and express command may both be lacking or uncertain, as the baptism of infants, necessary inference from the doctrine and commandments plainly set forth in Scripture may sufficiently warrant a practice of worship."[75]

Divine commands that are *expressly set down in Scripture* include such explicit commandments in the Bible as the First Commandment, requiring of us the worship of the God of the Bible alone, the Second Commandment, forbidding us to use graven images in our worship of God, the commands to read and preach the Word of God, to sing God's praises, to administer the sacraments, to receive offerings, and to make vows and oaths.

Divine commands that are *by good and necessary consequence deduced from Scripture* are as authoritative as statements *expressly set down in Scripture*.[76] "Conclusions fairly deduced from the declarations of the Word of God are as truly parts of Divine revelation as if they were expressly taught in the sacred volume."[77] This is the way Jesus proved the doctrine of resurrection against the Sadducees in Matthew 22:31–32, and the way Paul proved that Jesus is the Christ by reasoning with the Jews from the Old Testament in Acts 17:2–3. Furthermore, some of the most basic doctrines of the Christian faith are based on necessary inferences from express statements in the Bible, e.g., the doctrines of the Trinity, inerrancy, effectual calling, and infant baptism.

The church "has no commission to reason badly...logical inferences are not speculative opinions."[78] If we confine ourselves to the deduction of good and necessary consequences from the doctrines of the Bible, we will not evolve from those revealed truths the doctrines and traditions of man. Critics of the regulative principle of worship often base their case, not on logical and necessary inferences drawn from express statements in the Bible, but by "appealing to vague 'motifs' in Bible passages and then telling us (without biblical exegesis) that they are suggestive of some theological 'connection' or 'relation' (without definition)." Greg Bahnsen says : "To deal with broad and ambiguous allusions is not precise enough to demonstrate any specific conclusion; because there are no control principles or predictability in how such vague notions will be taken, the door is left open too wide for the interpreter's subjective creativity. The key to drawing artful 'connections' everywhere in the Bible, of course, is to make your categories broad and vague enough to include just about anything...That is the theologian supposed to do with such discussions? They aren't arguments really. They are more like mood enhancers."[79]

"All Scripture is...profitable for doctrine, for reproof, for correction, for instruction in righteousness." However, it cannot accomplish all these ends unless by the deduction of consequences. The apostle Paul understood the place of inference as is evident in his comments in Romans 8:9–13. After making several express statements about the Holy Spirit in the life of the believer in verses 9–11, he draws an inference from those statements in verses 12–13. When, in verse 12, he says, "So then, brethren..." he is deducing his conclusion from the teachings of verses 9–11. As Robert Shaw said: "Legitimate consequences, indeed, bring out the full meaning of the words of Scripture; and as we are endowed with the faculty of reason, and commanded to search the Scriptures, it was manifestly intended that we should draw conclusions from what is therein set down in express words."[80] Benjamin B. Warfield wrote: "It is the reformed contention, reflected here (in I, VI) by the Confession, that the sense of Scripture is Scripture, and that men are bound by its whole sense in all its implications."[81]

Honest and necessary conclusions drawn from the express statements of the Bible also include the use of approved historical examples recorded in the Bible in determining what God commands in worship. One example of this way of interpreting Scripture is concerning the change of the Sabbath from Saturday to Sunday with the resurrection of Jesus Christ. We have no express command to that effect, but we do have the example of Jesus Christ, who rested from His redemptive labors with His resurrection on the first day of the week, just as God rested from His creative labors on the seventh day of the week (Heb. 4:9–10). We also have the example of the apostles in the church in the books of Acts. The point is that divine example and Spirit-inspired apostolic example are as authoritative a guide as an express divine command. (For more on this subject see "William Cunningham on the Authority of Apostolic Example," pp. 170f.)

Thus, we are able to determine from the Bible what God has commanded us to do in our worship of Him by:

Express Commands

Approved Examples

Necessary Inferences

The Confessional statement of the regulative principle (I, VI) ends with this wise assertion, "There are some circumstances concerning the worship of God, and government of the Church, common to human actions and societies, which are to be ordered by the light of nature and Christian prudence, according to the general rules of the Word, which are always to be observed."

These *circumstances concerning the worship of God* are mere *circumstances*. They are *concerning* or *related to* the worship of God, but not *in* the worship of God. They do not have reference to anything pertaining to a person's worship of God. They do not pertain to any action or ritual that takes place as an ordinance of worship. *Circumstances* refer to those incidental things surrounding a worship service that have no spiritual significance. They do not pertain to the content or manner of worship. They are variables that can be altered or modified as need be. The fixed elements of worship, being commanded by God, may never be modified or altered.

These *circumstances* are things that are common to any serious, public group meeting of people. They include such things as the lighting, seating, time of meeting, place, and an almost infinite amount of individual circumstantial issues.

With reference to what is done in worship, the church's authority is limited to the administration of what God has commanded in the Bible. There is no discretion in this area, only to obey. But with reference to *some circumstances concerning the worship of God*, the church does have a measure of limited and well-defined discretion. In these areas, that are common concerns in any well-ordered, public assembly of people, the elders do have the discretion and duty to order and regulate them *by the light of nature and Christian prudence, according to the general rules of the Word of God*. This confessional statement means that in ordering the *circumstances* related to worship, the elders are to use:

1. Rational consideration of the needs and resources of the congregation

2. Wisdom in handling practical matters, exercising good judgment and common sense

3. Cautious consideration of the probable consequences and effects of their decision or action

4. Consistency with the general principles and implications of the Bible

As James Bannerman explains: "There are matters *not in* the public worship of God, *but about* the public worship of God . . . The *ceremonies* and institutions of Church worship are properly and distinctively matters *in sacris*, i.e., in sacred things, or in worship; the *circumstances* of Church worship, or those things that belong to it in common with the ordinary proceedings or peculiar solemnities of men, are properly and distinctively matters *circa sacra*, i.e., about sacred things, or about worship."[82]

> It is clear that circumstances which are common to human actions cannot by anything which is peculiar [unique] to church actions, and those which are common to human societies cannot be anything distinctive of the church as a certain kind of society. They are circumstances belonging to the temporal sphere—time, place, decorum, and the natural methods of discharging business which are necessities to all societies. The do not appertain to the kind of government [or worship] which the church ought to have, nor the mode in which it is to be dispensed.[83]

Girardeau goes on to quote James H. Thornwell of old Columbia Theological Seminary:

> In public worship, indeed in all commanded external actions, there are two elements—a fixed and a variable. The fixed element, involving the essence of a thing, is beyond the discretion of the church. The variable, involving only the circumstances of the action, its separable accidents, may be changed, modified or altered, according to the exigencies of the case.[84]

The apostle Paul says in 1 Corinthians 14:40. "Let all things be done properly and in an orderly manner." In other words, the church has the authority and the duty to maintain order and proper decorum in her assemblies and to restrain and correct any improprieties, indecencies, or disorder. Whenever the church uses this authority, it is not *in* public worship, it is *about* public worship, i.e., it is not a part of worship, it is in connection with worship. This discretionary authority is with reference to *circumstances* not ceremonies. In carrying out Paul's exhortation "the Church received no authority from the apostle to exercise jurisdiction within the territory belonging to the worship of God, but only authority to exercise jurisdiction in a territory connected indeed with the circumstances of worship, but really belonging to reason and nature."[85]

Although a broad line of demarcation separates the church's authority *in* worship from its authority *about* or surrounding worship, this discretionary authority of the church, in the circumstances, has been abused by the church in the past. From this abuse the church has usurped the power of discretion in the actual worship of God, leading to innovations in worship, and failing to distinguish commanded *elements* in worship from *circumstances* relating to worship. Especially today do we find people using the language of the *Westminster Confession of Faith* "to cover a multitude of sins." They blur the great difference between the commanded elements in worship and the circumstances about worship to justify the introduction of all kinds of human innovations in the worship of God. They always have something new but not commanded by God: a two hundred-balloon salute to God to begin the worship service, or the serving of communion by the elders wearing white robes.

"In what belongs strictly to the institutions and ceremonies of worship the Church has no authority, except to dispense them as Christ has prescribed. In what belongs to the circumstances of worship necessary to its being dispensed with propriety, and so as to avoid confusion, the Church has the authority to regulate them as nature and reason (and the implications of the Word of God) prescribe."[86]

Where should the line be drawn between ceremonies and circumstances? How are we to distinguish between them?

1. Ceremonies or elements in worship have been given by God in the Bible either by express command, approved example, or necessary inference.

2. Circumstances are mere circumstances. They are non-essential, incidental, of no spiritual value, no sanctifying power, and no symbolic significance as a visual aid to worship. To raise a circumstance to a ceremony is to attribute to it a spiritual significance God has not given to it.

3. Circumstances cannot be determined directly by the Bible. This is not a denial of the all-sufficiency of the Bible. Rather, it is simply to say that the Bible does not concern itself with all these circumstances. Because their number is almost infinite—time, place, language, décor, *ad infinitum*—if the Bible contained them, it would be millions of pages in length. If the Bible defines a specific principle, however, it is not a circumstance. Furthermore, only God has the prerogative to make a circumstance an element of worship.

4. Circumstances are those issues that are necessary to the organizing and decorum of any serious and public assembly of people.

5. Elements in worship, being commanded by God, are not optional. Circumstances can be changed, eliminated, or added without consequence to public worship. For example, a church might decide to exclude air conditioning from its sanctuary, but it most certainly may not decide to exclude prayer.

6. Although elders have discretion in the circumstances, even then, when they use this authority, they must do so prudently and only when necessary. They elders must present good and wise reasons to the congregation for their decision. It is often difficult for godly people to submit themselves to regulations and guidelines that they do not perceive to be right, useful or necessary.[87]

George Gillespie, a Scottish Presbyterian minister at the Westminster Assembly, in his book, *A Dispute Against the English Popish Ceremonies*, gives us three marks by which they may be distinguished,[88] (which marks are interspersed here with quotes from James Bannerman).[89]

> The matter must be only a circumstance of Divine worship, and no substantial part of it—no sacred, significant, and efficacious ceremony.[90]

> That which the church may lawfully prescribe by her laws and ordinances, as a thing left to her determination, must be one of such things as were not determinable by Scripture . . . because individual are infinita. We mean not in any wise to circumscribe the infinite power and wisdom of God, only we speak upon supposition of the bounds and limits which God did set to His written Word, within which He would have it contained, and over which He thought fit that it should not exceed. The case being thus put, as it is, we say truly of those several and changeable circumstances (individual) which are left to the determination of the church, that, being almost infinite (infinita), they were not particularly determinable in Scripture; for the particular definition of those occurring circumstances which were to be rightly ordered in the works of God's service to the end of the world, and that ever according to the exigency (need) of every present occasion and different case, should have filled the whole world with books.[91]

> If the church prescribe anything lawfully, so that she prescribe no more than she has power given her to prescribe, her ordinance must be accompanied with some good reason and warrant given for the satisfaction of tender consciences.[92]

> There must be a sufficient reason, in the way of securing decency or preventing disorder, to warrant the Church in enacting regulations even in the circumstances of worship as contradistinguished from its ceremonies. Without some necessity laid upon it, and a sufficient reason to state for its procedure, the Church has no warrant to encroach upon the liberty of its members. Even in matters lawful and indifferent, not belonging to Divine worship itself, but to the circumstances of it, the Church is bound to show a necessity or a sufficient reason for its enactments.[93]

But such tests as these, it is not a matter of much difficulty practically to determine what matters connected with the worship of God are, and what are not, within the apostolic canon, Let all things be done decently and in order. They are the very things which reason is competent to regulate, which cannot be determined for all times and places by Scripture; which belong not to the Church worship itself, but to the circumstances or accompaniments common to it with civil solemnities, and which must be ordered in the Church, as in any other society, so as to secure decency and to prevent confusion.[94]

John L. Girardeau has given us this further helpful explanation of the criteria by which we identify mere circumstances surrounding worship, after which he applies his explanation to "prescribed liturgies."

There are three criteria by which the kind of circumstances attending worship which fall under the discretionary power of the church may be determined: first, they are not qualities or modes of the acts of worship; they are extraneous to them as a certain kind of actions; secondly, they are common to the acts of all societies, and, therefore, not peculiar [unique] to the acts of the church as a particular sort of society—they are not characteristic and distinctive of her acts and predicable of them alone; and thirdly, they are conditions necessary to the performance of the acts of worship— without them the acts of this society could not be done, as without them the acts of no society could be done.

Let us now bring a liturgy to the test of these criteria . . . It cannot abide the first, because it qualifies and modifies the act of prayer itself—it is a kind of prayer, a mode in which it is offered. It cannot abide the second, because it is not common to human actions and societies . . . It cannot abide the third, because a liturgy is not a condition necessary to the performance of the act of prayer. Its necessary could only be pleaded on one of two ground: either that without it the act of prayer cannot be performed at all, and that is out of the question; or, that without it the act cannot be performed decently and in order, and to take that ground is to impeach the office of the Holy Spirit, who is specially promised to teach us how to pray and what things to pray for...[95]

Therefore, Bryan Schwertley concludes: "The attempt to broaden the definition of the circumstances of worship, or to blur the distinction between worship elements and circumstances, or to merge distinct elements into broad categories, is unscriptural and anti-confessional. One must never treat the elements of worship as abstractions that can be molded to fit one's own preconceptions of what is permissible in worship. The proper biblical interpretive procedure lets the Bible tell us what the distinct elements of worship are and lets Scripture delineate the rules for each element."[96]

One critic of the regulative principle rejects the Confession's concept of *circumstances* of worship in favor of his new term "applications," and then uses this innovation to "make" the Confession mean what it does not mean, when interpreted according to the original intent of its authors. Therefore, he can conclude that although the Bible tells us what to do in worship generally, it leaves it to us "to determine the specifics by our own sanctified wisdom, according to the general rules of the Word. Determining the specifics is what I call 'application.'"[97]

Once again, as he has so admirably done with other detractors of the regulative principle of worship, Brian Schwertley easily exposes the weakness of this critic's argument in his article, "The Neo-Presbyterian Challenge."

> First, Frame's contention that some (unnamed) Puritans and Scottish Presbyterians regarded circumstances as secular [as Frame alleges] is wrong and misleading. They did not regard the circumstances of worship as secular or religiously neutral. They did, however, regard them as things that were not specifically determinable by Scripture, that had a certain commonality with civil or secular affairs. For example, a civil meeting will have a beginning and end, chairs, lighting, podium . . . However, these circumstances of worship are to be designed or conducted "according to the general rules of Scripture." (p. 23)

> Second, Frame gives us an over-simplification of the concept of circumstances in order to make the confessional understanding look incompetent and unworkable. Frame

tells us that since the words we use in prayer are of "great spiritual importance" and prayer is not "common to human actions and societies"; therefore, we need a better more workable concept than the term 'circumstances' of worship. Frame's alternative is 'applications.'—Is what believers do when they pray merely a circumstance of worship?—The Westminster divines did not regard the content of prayer in the same manner as the type of seating, lighting, pulpit style, flooring, etc. Therefore, the idea of choosing one's own words for prayer in worship renders the concept of circumstances of worship somehow unworkable is not true. (pp. 23–24)

If one holds to the confessional understanding of the regulative principle, that all the parts or elements of worship require divine warrant, one must explain those things that are necessary to conduct a public meeting that are not specifically addressed in Scripture. Are there not areas related to a public worship service that do not directly affect the content or parts of religious worship? The confessional answer that there are some circumstances relating to worship that are not themselves part of worship or worship ordinances is unavoidable and obvious. If Frame observes that in certain areas or applications the concept of circumstances need clarification, that is one thing. But why does he insist on tossing it aside for his own concept of applications? The main reason is related to Frame's rejection of the confessional doctrine of elements or parts of religious worship each of which requires divine warrant. Once one rejects the concept of worship elements, [e.g., prayer, praise, reading the Bible, preaching the Bible, administration of the sacraments, receiving the offering, etc.], one is left only with broad categories...Frame has taken the concept of "the general rules of the Word" that the Westminster divines only applied to the circumstances of worship and has applied it to worship itself. This incredible broadening of the concept of divine warrant renders the whole section in the Confession dealing with the circumstances of worship superfluous. Since Frame has already taken the Confession's "the general rules of the Word" and applied it to worship itself, he must redefine the circumstances into applications. Why? Because the term "applications" is broad enough to cover everything relating to worship, whether worship ordinance or the circumstantial areas. In fact everything in life that we do as Christians is an application of Scripture in some sense. Frame continues on his path of taking well thought-out clear distinctions found in the Westminster Standards and replacing them with very general concepts. Remember, the end game is human autonomy in worship. (p. 24)

I can do no better in concluding this section of our consideration of the regulative principle of worship than by quoting Brian Schwertley, James Thornwell, and John L. Girardeau:

The regulative principle of worship (i.e., truly reformed worship) is the only principle that can withstand all exegetical attacks and stem today's sweeping tide of human worship innovations. It can withstand all exegetical attacks because it is founded upon the sacred Scripture and nothing else. It can stem the tide of human innovation in worship because it cuts off, at the root, all innovation, all human tradition and will-worship. The seeds of will-worship are killed before they can sprout. Humanly originated worship traditions are forbidden at the outset, and are thus not given the opportunity of taking root and displacing that worship which God has instituted. Everything in worship must have a divine warrant, i.e., it must be proved from the word of God. (Bryan Schwertley)[98]

As under the Old Dispensation nothing connected with the worship or discipline of the Church of God was left to the wisdom or discretion of man, but everything was accurately prescribed by the authority of God, so, under the New, no voice is to be heard in the household of faith but the voice of the Son of God. The power of the church is purely ministerial and declarative. She is only to hold forth the doctrine, enforce the laws and execute the government which Christ has given her. She is to add nothing of her own to, and to subtract nothing from, what her Lord has established. Discretionary power she does not possess. (James H. Thornwell)[99]

I would ask the critics of the regulative principle of worship: Why would anyone want to add to what God has commanded for worship? What is so restrictive about the reformed and biblical regulative principle of worship? Why have you so easily discarded a principle that has guided the church so effectively in her worship for almost five hundred years? What do you want do in the worship of God that you cannot do under the regulative principle? Where did that practice or rite that you want originate: in the brain of man or in the mind of God? Why do you think that the things you want to do in worship that are not commanded in the Bible are things God wants you to do in your worship of Him?

> Let us endeavor, by grace, to make this church as perfect a specimen of Scriptural truth, order and worship as the imperfections of the present state will permit. Let us take her by the hand and lead her to the Word alone. Let us pass the Reformers, let us pass the Fathers, uncovering our heads to them in token of our profound appreciation of their labors for truth, and heartily receiving from them all they speak in accordance with the Word; but let us pass on and pause not, until with our sacred charge we read the Oracles of God, and with her bow at the Master's feet, and listen to the Master's voice. Let obedience to the Word of Christ in all things be the law of her life; so that when the day of review shall come, and section after section of the universal church shall halt for judgment before the great Inspector Himself, although, no doubt, there will be much of unfaithfulness of life that will draw on His forgiveness, His eye may detect no departure from His Word in her principles, her order and her worship. (John L. Girardeau)[100]

CHAPTER THREE

THE SECOND COMMANDMENT AND THE REGULATIVE PRINCIPLE OF WORSHIP

> You shall not make for yourself an idol, or any likeness of
> what is in heaven above or on the earth beneath or in the
> water under the earth. You shall not worship them or serve
> them; for I, the Lord your God, am a jealous God, visiting
> the iniquity of the fathers on the children, on the third and
> fourth generations of those who hate Me, but showing
> lovingkindness to thousands, to those who love Me and keep
> My commandments. (Exodus 20:4–6)

The Second Commandment cannot be understood
correctly apart from its inseparable connection to the First
Commandment—"You shall have no other gods before Me"
(Ex. 20:3). In the First Commandment we are instructed to
worship and serve Jehovah alone; in the Second
Commandment we are instructed to worship and serve Jehovah
alone, only by the way in which He has commanded us to
worship Him. The First Commandment is concerned with the
object of our worship; the Second Commandment is concerned
with the manner of our worship. The First tells us Whom to
worship and the Second tells us how to worship Him. "First
there is faith in God and no other god; then there is an
application of this faith into action (or better, inaction: no
graven images). The Second Commandment is an application
of the principle governing the First Commandment."[101]

The Second Commandment in Exodus 20:4–6 is comprised of a prohibition, a declaration of God's perfections, and a sanction. The prohibition is twofold and the sanction is twofold. The two prohibitions are: (1) Do not make for yourselves idols and graven images; and (2) Do not worship these graven images or God by means of these images. In the declaration of God's perfections, God reveals to us that He is the Lord your God and that He is a jealous God. The sanctions include a curse and a blessing: (1) The curse: God will visit with judgment the iniquity of the fathers on the children, to the third and forth generations of those who hate Him; and (2). The blessing: God will show lovingkindness to thousands, to those who love Him and keep His commandments.

Why does God hate graven images? Why is His anger so severe and so abiding on those who break the Second Commandment? Here are several reasons:

They represent an attempt to control God.

They are rooted in a theology of magic.

Their goal is the creation of a satanic world order.

They deny the spirituality of God.

They deny the freedom and sovereignty of God.

They deny the majesty of God.

They deny the covenant of God.

The concern of the Second Commandment is primarily with the worship of God, (although it also relates to politics, as we shall see in the future). More specifically, it deals with the manner in which God wants to be worshipped. Just as God alone is to be worshipped, so He is to be worshipped only as He has prescribed in His Word. As John Calvin wrote: "It is unnecessary to parade our 'good intentions' as a coverup for what we have invented, indeed; but on the contrary we should know that the principal service which God requires is obedience."[102]

Our sovereign Lord God wants to be worshipped and served according to what pleases Him, with worship that is consistent with His character and will. In His Word He has revealed to us His character and His will and how it pleases Him for us to worship Him. "It is neither a matter of indifference to God as to how we serve Him, nor ought we to be of the opinion that He will be pleased just so long as He is served, even if it is in a manner which is acceptable to us. No, He wishes to be served in a manner pleasing to Him and which He has prescribed to us."[103]

As Calvin again states:

We see that He pronounces a horrible sentence of condemnation on all who allow themselves to be governed by their [own] opinion. They would say, of course, (and such is the case), that they mean to worship God. But how? He does not at all accept such worship. Rather He despises it and considers it detestable. Thus we are instructed in this passage not to undertake what might seem good to us. And above all, when it is a matter of worshipping God, we are not to give any attention whatever to our own imagination. But we are to follow in all simplicity what He has ordained in His Word, without adding anything to it at all. For as soon as we fall away from that, however slightly, whatever case we might cite, and try to justify ourselves, God will surely punish us. [104]

In forbidding the most extreme corruption of the homage and worship we give the one true God,—the worship of images—God is forbidding all manner of worship of Him that is inconsistent with His character and His revealed will. It requires of us whatever manner of worship God has commanded in His Word and prohibits all others, for it is His prerogative to reveal Himself to us, just as He has done. [105]

The *Westminster Larger Catechism* gives us a wise and thorough exposition of the demands and prohibitions of the Second Commandment.

The duties required in the second commandment are, the receiving, observing, and keeping pure and entire, all such religious worship and ordinances as God hath instituted in

83

His word; particularly prayer and thanksgiving in the name of Christ; the reading, preaching, and hearing of the word; the administration and receiving of the sacraments; church government and discipline; the ministry and maintenance thereof; religious fasting; swearing by the name of God, and vowing unto Him: as also the disapproving, detesting, opposing, all false worship; and, according to each one's place and calling, removing it, and all monuments of idolatry. (Q. 108)

The sins forbidden in the second commandment are, all devising, counseling, commanding, using, and any wise approving, any religious worship not instituted by God Himself; tolerating a false religion; the making any representation of God, of all or of any of the three persons, either inwardly in our mind, or outwardly in any kind of image or likeness of any creature whatsoever; all worshipping of it, or God in it or by it; the making of any representation of feigned deities, and all worship of them, or service belonging to them; all superstitious devices, corrupting the worship of God, adding to it, or taking from it, whether invented and taken up of ourselves, or received by tradition from others, though under the title of antiquity, custom, devotion, good intent, or any other pretence whatsoever; simony; sacrilege; all neglect, contempt, hindering, and opposing the worship and ordinances which God hath appointed. (Q. 109)

CHAPTER FOUR

The Great Commission and the Regulative Principle of Worship

As the resurrected Lord Jesus Christ ascended into heaven, He gave His church this great commission, "Go therefore and make disciples of all the nations, baptizing them in the name of the Father and the Son and the Holy Spirit, teaching them to observe all that I commanded you" (Matt. 28:19–20). The last line is pertinent to our understanding of the regulative principle of worship. The great 17th Century Puritan exegete, John Owen, explains:

> In things which concern the worship of God, the commanding power is Christ; and His command the adequate rule and measure of our obedience. The teaching, commanding and enjoining of others to do and observe these commands, is the duty of those entrusted with Christ's authority under Him. Their commission to teach and enjoin, and our duty to do and observe, have the same rules, the same measure, bounds and limits. What they teach and enjoin beyond what Christ has commanded, they do it not by virtue of any commission from Him; what we do beyond what He has commanded, we do it not in obedience to Him; what they so teach, they do it in their own name, not His; what we so do, we do in our own strength, not His, nor to His glory.

The things our Savior treats about are principally the "agenda" of the gospel, things to be done and observed in the worship of God. Of these, as was said, He makes His own command the adequate rule and measure. "Teach men to observe *panta osa* all whatsoever I command," in their so doing alone, does He promise His presence with them, that is, to enable them unto the discharge of their duty. He commands, I say, all that shall to the end of the world be called to serve Him in the work of the gospel, to teach. In that expression He comprises their whole duty, as their whole authority is given them in this commission. In their teaching, indeed, they are to command with all authority; and upon the non-obedience of men unto their teaching, either by not receiving their word, or by walking unworthy of it when it is received in the profession of it, He has allotted them the course of their whole proceedings; but still requiring that all be regulated by what they are originally commissioned and enabled to teach and command. Let then the imposition of a liturgy be tried by this rule. It was never by Christ commanded to His apostles, cannot by any be taught as His command, and therefore men, in the teaching or imposing of it, have no promise of His presence, nor do they that observe it, yield any obedience unto Him therein. This I am sure will be the rule of Christ's inquiry at His great visitation at the last day; the things which Himself has commanded will be inquired after, as to some men's teachings, and all men's observation, and those only. And I cannot but admire with what peace and satisfaction to their own souls, men can pretend to act as by commission from Christ, as the chief administrators of His gospel and worship on the earth, and make it their whole business almost to teach men to do and observe what He never commanded.[106]

The Great Commission of Jesus Christ calls the Church to the evangelization of the world, making the nations Christ's disciples, and gathering and perfecting the elect by means of the Word of God empowered by the Holy Spirit. We move forward in the authority of Him who said that "all authority has been given to Me in heaven and on earth;" and as we are faithful we are guaranteed success by His promise, "And lo, I am with you always, even to the end of the age" (Matt. 28:18, 20).

In all our aggressive evangelism, we must never forget that "the church is not only the divinely-commissioned publisher, she is also the divinely-commanded conservator, of the truth. Conservatism and aggressiveness are twin duties, complementary of each other. It is just as important to maintain the truth as it is to propagate it. The danger is that the church will neglect the former duty in discharging the latter—that she will be more solicitous to preach the gospel in some form to the world than to guard the particular type of it which she impresses on the forming and infantile churches of converted heathen men. In her onward march the church cannot afford to neglect her base line. As we value the vital interests of our own organization as well as of those established abroad, we must see to it, with sedulous and unremitting vigilance, that we keep ourselves conformed in all things to the will of Christ as revealed in the sacred word.

"We are not without peril . . . there is in the best churches of Protestantism [today] a growing latitudinarianism [liberalism] which spurns the restraints of a complete and ultimate rule of faith and duty... Depend upon it, there are defections and there are struggles before us."[107] What then is the course we must set for ourselves? "...[L]et conformity to the Word be the law of [the church's] development [and advance]—conformity to the Word, close, implicit, undeviating in doctrine, government and worship."[108]

CHAPTER FIVE

THE ELEMENTS OF WORSHIP

Elements of Worship are *parts of the ordinary religious worship of God*, (WCF 21:5). They are all the specific things we do in our worship of God because they are commanded by God in the Bible.

Some pastors inside the reformed camp hold the view that the Westminster Standards are wrong in requiring divine commands for specific parts of worship. They say that all the Bible does is give us "broad theological generalities" and that we ought to use our "sanctified wisdom" to "apply the generalities," with creative innovation and "considerable flexibility." This viewpoint allows for a wide variety of worship practices as long as they can in some way be "connected" with the generalities of the Bible.

There are many problems with this view. First, these "applications" of the Bible's broad generalities all originate with man's "sanctified wisdom." However, God repudiates all worship practices that originate with man, Christian or non-Christian, as we have seen. Second, this view can approve almost any innovation in worship and is being used to justify dramas, skits, times for greeting each other during the worship service, and various other human inventions. Those who hold these views take things in the Bible that have nothing to do with public worship, find some vague, loose, and undefined "connection" to worship, and make subjective applications. Third, this view contradicts the biblical teaching that all the specific parts of worship require specific commands from God—express directives, approved examples, or necessary inferences. We have established that Deuteronomy 12:32 governs all worship under the New Covenant; therefore, in the worship of God, we are to do carefully whatever *God* commands us with no additions or subtractions.

Those who want to cast aside the regulative principle of worship argue that "Scripture does not give us a list of elements required for Christian worship services." Schwertley responds by describing that claim as a "disingenuous and inconsistent method of argumentation . . . Although there is no detailed list set forth in the New Testament of worship elements, the various elements or parts of religious worship are easily proved from divine imperatives and descriptions of worship services or approved historical examples found in Scripture."[109]

The elements of worship that are commanded by God in the Bible include:

PRAYING:

> O You who hear prayer,
> To You all Men come. (Psalm 65:2)

> Hear my cry, O God;
> Give heed to my prayer.
> From the end of the earth I call to You
> when my heart is faint;
> Lead me to the rock that is higher than I.
> For You have been a refuge for me,
> A tower of strength against the enemy. (Psalm 61:1–3)

> Trust in Him at all times, O people;
> Pour out your heart before Him;
> God is a refuge for us. (Psalm 62:8)

> (These Psalms all begin with the heading, "For the choir director," thus indicating that they were prayers used in temple worship.)

READING THE BIBLE:

For Moses from ancient generations has in every city those who preach him, since he is read in the synagogues every Sabbath. (Acts 15:21)

Blessed is he who reads and those who hear the words of the prophecy, and heed the things which are written in it (Revelation 1:3)

And all the people gathered as one man at the square . . . and they asked Ezra the scribe to bring the book of the Law of Moses which the Lord had given Israel...Ezra the scribe stood at a wooden podium which they had made for that purpose...Ezra opened the book in the sight of all the people for he was standing above all the people; and when he opened it, all the people stood up. (Nehemiah 8:1–5)

I adjure you by the Lord to have this letter read to all the brethren. (1 Thessalonians 5:27)

When this letter is read among you, have it also read in the church of the Laodiceans; and you, for your part read my letter that is coming from Laodicea. (Colossians 4:16)

PREACHING THE BIBLE:

Then Ezra blessed the Lord the great God...Also Jeshua, Bani, Sherebiah...and the Levites explained the law to the people while the people remained in their place. They read from the book, from the law of God, translating to give the sense so that they understood the reading. (Nehemiah 8:6–8)

They were continually devoting themselves to the apostles' teaching and to fellowship, to the breaking of bread and to prayer. (Acts 2:42)

But during the night an angel of the Lord opened the gates of the prison, and taking them out he said: "Go, stand and speak to the people in the Temple the whole message of this Life." Upon hearing this, they entered into the Temple about daybreak and began to teach. (Acts 5:19–21)

When they reached Salamis, they began to proclaim the word of God in the synagogues of the Jews. (Acts 13:5)

And on the first day of the week, when we were gathered together to break bread, Paul began talking to them, intending to depart the next day, and he prolonged his message [logon] until midnight. (Acts 20:7)

And when I came to you, brethren, I did not come with superiority of speech or of wisdom, proclaiming to you the testimony of God. For I determined to know nothing among you except Jesus Christ, and Him crucified. And I was with you in weakness and in fear and in much trembling, and my message and my preaching were not in persuasive words of wisdom, but in demonstration of the Spirit and of power, so that your faith should not rest on the wisdom of men, but on the power of God. (1 Corinthians 2:1–5)

Administrating of the Sacraments of Baptism and Lord's Supper:

And Jesus came up and spoke to them, saying, "All authority has been given to Me in heaven and on earth. Go therefore and make disciples of all the nations, baptizing them in the name of the Father and the Son and the Holy Spirit, teaching them to observe all that I commanded you; and lo, I am with you always, even to the end of the age." (Matthew 28:18–20)

Therefore when you meet together, it is not to eat the Lord's Supper, for in your eating each one takes his own supper first; and one is hungry and another is drunk. What! Do you not have houses in which to eat and drink? Or do you despise the church of God, and shame those who have nothing? (1 Corinthians 11:20–21)

They were continually devoting themselves to the apostles' teaching and to fellowship, to the breaking of bread and to prayer. (Acts 2:42)

Singing of God's Praises:

(For the choir director.)
Shout joyfully to God, all the earth;
Sing the glory of His name;
Make His praise glorious...

All the earth will worship You,
And will sing praises to You. (Psalm 66:1–4)

(For the choir director.)
O clap your hands, all peoples;
Shout to God with the voice of joy.
For the Lord Most High is to be feared,
A great King over all the earth. (Psalm 47:1–2)

WITH MUSICAL INSTRUMENTS:

Praise the Lord!
Praise God in His sanctuary; . . .
Praise Him with trumpet sound;
Praise Him with harp and lyre.
Praise Him with timbrel and dancing;
Praise Him with stringed instruments and pipe.
Praise Him with loud cymbals;
Praise Him with resounding cymbals.
Let everything that has breath praise the Lord.
Praise the Lord. (Psalm 150:1, 3–6)

WITH PSALMS, HYMNS AND SPIRITUAL SONGS:

Let the word of Christ richly dwell within you; with all
wisdom teaching and admonishing one another with psalms
and hymns and spiritual songs, singing with thankfulness in
your hearts to God. (Colossians 3:16)

GIVING OF TITHES AND OFFERINGS:

Ascribe to the Lord the glory of His name;
Bring an offering, and come into His courts. (Psalm 96:8)

Now concerning the collection for the saints, as I directed
the churches of Galatia, so do you also. On the first day of
every week each one of you is to put aside and save, as he
may prosper, so that no collections be made when I come. (1
Corinthians 16:1–2)

TAKING OATHS AND VOWS:

Offer to God a sacrifice of thanksgiving,
And pay your vows to the Most High. (Psalm 50:14)

I shall come into Your house with burnt offerings;
I shall pay You my vows. (Psalm 66:13)

You stand today, all of you, before the Lord your God . . .
that you may enter into the covenant with the Lord your
God, and into His oath which the Lord your God is making
with you today, in order that He may establish you today as
His people and that He may be your God. (Deuteronomy
29:10–13)

CONFESSING OF THE FAITH:

You shall fear only the Lord your God; and you shall
worship Him, and swear by His name. You shall not follow
other gods, any of the gods of the peoples who surround you,
for the Lord your God in the midst of you is a jealous God.
(Deuteronomy 6:13–15)

John Calvin explains how the command to swear by God's
name in His worship is a command to confess our faith in Him.
He shows that swearing by God's name is in reality a
confessing of our faith. "For we have seen heretofore, that such
as swear (I mean as they ought to swear) do take their oath by
the name of God, because that only He is the sufficient witness
of the truth, and will judge all such as turn His truth into [a
license to sin]. And so in this text Moses shows again that when
we have worshipped God, we must also make a declaration of
our faith, for as men may perceive us to be His people, and that
He reigns among us, that we be free from all superstition and
idolatry, and that we hold none other religion than that which
the living God has given us...

"Now seeing it is so that he which swears does call God to
witness, and also submits himself to punishment if he shall have
abused His holy and sacred name, is it not a doing of homage
unto God? For our swearing by Him is because He has
sovereign dominion over us, because it belongs to Him to
search our hearts, because He must be our judge, and because
we must yield account of our whole life before Him...

"By reason whereof we are commanded, not only to swear by the name of God, but also to yield such confession of Him before men, as we may show ourselves to be His people in deed, and that we would [desire] that He should reign among us, and that His name should be glorified...When Moses said that we must swear by the name of God, it is as much as if he should say, my friends, like as you worship the Lord, so must you also maintain His honor among men. In so much that if any man will compel you to transform or change your religion, you shall not [allow] it in any case whatsoever; but stand [firm] in this uncorruptness to say, we have the one God who has called us to Him, and both created and redeemed us, and therefore it is good reason that we should be His heritage, and continue wholly His."[110]

> If you confess with your mouth, "Jesus as Lord," and believe in your heart that God raised Him from the dead, you shall be saved. (Romans 10:9)

Pronouncing the Benediction:

> Then the Lord spoke to Moses, saying, "Speak to Aaron and to his sons, saying, 'Thus you shall bless the sons of Israel, you shall say to them: "The Lord bless you, and keep you; the Lord make His face shine on you, And be gracious to you; the Lord lift up His countenance on you, and give you peace.' "So they shall invoke My name on the sons of Israel, and I then will bless them." (Numbers 6:22–27)

> The grace of the Lord Jesus Christ, and the love of God, and the fellowship of the Holy Spirit, be with you all. (2 Corinthians 13:14)

Exercising Church Discipline:

> For I, on my part, though absent in body but present in spirit, have already judged him who has so committed this, as though I were present. In the name of our Lord Jesus, when you are assembled, and I with you in spirit, with the power of our Lord Jesus, I have decided to deliver such a one to Satan for the destruction of his flesh, that his spirit may be saved in the day of the Lord Jesus. (1 Corinthians 5:3–5)

Saying a Congregational Amen:

Then Ezra blessed the Lord the great God. And all the people answered, "Amen, Amen!" while lifting up their hands; then they bowed low and worshipped the Lord with their faces to the ground. (Nehemiah 8:6)

Blessed be the Lord, the God of Israel,
From everlasting even to everlasting.
Then all the people said, "Amen," and praised the Lord.
(1 Chronicles 16:36)

Blessed be the Lord, the God of Israel,
From everlasting even to everlasting.
And let all the people say, "Amen."
Praise the Lord. (Psalm 106:48)

Fasting:

Whenever you fast, do not put on a gloomy face as the hypocrites do; for they neglect their appearance in order to be seen fasting by men. Truly I say to you, they have their reward in full. But you, when you fast, anoint your head, and wash your face; so that your fasting may not be noticed by men, but by your Father who is in secret; and your Father who sees what is done in secret will reward you. (Matthew 6:16–17)

Scheduling Special Days of Thanksgiving:

On those days the Jews rid themselves of their enemies, and it was a month which was turned for them from sorrow into gladness and from mourning into a good day; that they should make them days of feasting and rejoicing and sending portions of food to one another and gifts to the poor. (Esther 9:22)[111]

Oh give thanks to the Lord for He is good;
For His lovingkindness is everlasting.
Let the redeemed of the Lord say so,
Whom He has redeemed from the hand of the adversary,
And gathered from the lands,
From the east and from the west,
From the north and from the south. (Psalm 107:1–3)

We have seen the specific things God wants us to do in our worship of Him as commanded in the Bible. Can you think of anything else we ought to do in worship? Can you think of anything else God left out that He should have commanded us? Do you know of any other rites or rituals of spiritual significance and religious symbolism that would make our worship more meaningful and complete *beside* what God has commanded? Maybe God just forgot to mention some things He would like for us to add?

To ask these questions is to answer them. To answer them in the affirmative would be blasphemous, for it would dishonor the wisdom and sovereignty of God and exalt the opinion and traditions of man. That is a direct contradiction of what God is doing today. "The pride of man will be humbled, and the loftiness of man will be abased, and the LORD alone will be exalted on that day...before the terror of the LORD and the splendor of His majesty ...[Therefore] stop regarding man, whose breath of life is in his nostrils, for why should he be esteemed?" (Isaiah 2:17, 21, 22)

> Do not add to His words, or He will reprove you, and you
> will be proved a liar. (Proverbs 30:6)

CHAPTER SIX

COMMON OBJECTIONS TO THE REGULATIVE PRINCIPLE OF WORSHIP

One of the historical distinctives of biblical and reformed Presbyterianism has been our regulative principle of worship (Deuteronomy 12:32). It has always had its critics. In the seventeenth and eighteenth centuries the Lutherans and Anglicans apposed it. In the nineteenth century many revivalists rejected it. In the twentieth century, charismatics and fundamentalists ignored or opposed the regulative principle. In the late twentieth century and early twenty-first century, the opposition has come from within the reformed camp. We now turn to address the arguments of these last objectors.

Most objections to the Bible's regulative principle of worship are based on inadequate exegesis of Bible texts, misunderstandings, misrepresentations, and speculations. I have previously attempted to answer some of the objections brought against the regulative principle of worship. I will review previous arguments and address some new concerns.

1. The argument that Deuteronomy 4:2 cannot be used to support the regulative principle of worship because it is too broad and comprehensive.[112]

2. The argument that because "all of life is worship" therefore Deuteronomy 4:2 cannot be used for support.

The latter argument states that since all of life is worship, and since life has many facets not strictly regulated by the Bible (e.g., mowing the lawn, brushing teeth), therefore, worship, being life-wide, is not regulated either. While it is true that we are to do all to the glory of God (1 Corinthians 10:31), that in everything we do we are to live to the Lord (Romans 14:7–8), and that we are to present ourselves as living sacrifices to God (Romans 12:1), "the idea that all of life is worship and therefore no distinction exists between public worship and activities like mowing the lawn is absurd. There are several reasons why we must regard 'the all-of-life-is-worship' argument as unscriptural."[113]

First, there are several passages from both the Old and New Testaments that teach and/or assume that public worship is special and set apart from everyday life [e.g., Psalm 22:22, 25[114]; 27:4[115]; 84:1–2[116]; 87:2[117]; Ecclesiastes 5:1–2[118]; Leviticus 23:3; Acts 15:21; Hebrews 10:24–25]. ...

Second, Christ the king and head of the church has appointed public officers with special public functions that require a special public use, [e.g., Ephesians 4:8, 11, 12]. ...

Third, when the apostle Paul discusses the conduct of believers during public worship, he sets forth regulations that presuppose a sharp distinction between public worship and all of life. For example, women may speak at a barbecue and may teach their children during home school, yet they are strictly forbidden to speak or teach during the public worship service, (cf. 1 Corinthians 14:34; 1 Timothy 2:12–14). Regarding the Lord 's Supper, Paul tells believers that they must conduct themselves in a proper manner when coming to the Lord's table (1 Cor. 11:17–34). The regulations regarding this sacrament obviously do not apply to the local picnic or volleyball game. ...

Fourth, the term for church (*ekklesia*) often denotes a society of professing Christians who constitute a local church that meets together for public worship in a particular location

(Act. 5:11, 11:26, 1 Cor. 11:18, 16:19, Rom. 16:23, Gal. 1:2, 1 Thes. 2:14, Col. 4:15, Phm. 2, Rev. 1:11, etc.). ...

The New Testament church met together for public worship on the Lord's Day (Acts 2:1, 20:7, 1 Cor. 23, 26, 34, 35, 16:1, 2). Lord's Day worship was commanded by God (Lev. 23:3, Heb. 10:24–25). It is a period of time set apart from every day life. Public worship consists of certain elements that are authorized by Scripture such as: reading the Scriptures... prayer...preaching from the Bible...the administration of the sacraments...and the singing of Psalms. It clearly would be inappropriate to treat public worship conducted by the church in the same manner as areas of life that are indifferent...

Fifth, the Bible teaches that there is a special presence of God in public worship. ...

Clarkson writes:

'The Lord has engaged to be with every particular saint, but when the particulars are joined in public worship, there are all the engagements united together. The Lord engages himself to let forth as it were, a stream of his comfortable, quickening presence to every particular person that fears him, but when many of these particulars join together to worship God, then these streams are united and meet in one. So that the presence of God, which, enjoyed in private, is but a stream, in public becomes a river, a river that makes glad the city of God.' ...To argue that all of life is worship and thus public worship is not strictly regulated by God's word is akin to comparing the Lord's Supper to that which is common or profane.'[119]

The *Westminster Confession of Faith* stands against this "all-of-life-is-worship" argument. In XXI, VI, it says that "God is to be worshipped everywhere in spirit and in truth; as in private families daily, and in secret each one by himself; so more solemnly in the public assemblies, which are not carelessly or willfully to be neglected or forsaken, when God, by His Word or providence, calleth thereunto." The people of God may worship God anywhere, as long as they do so *in spirit and in truth*. And, although they are to have times of family worship *daily*, along with regular times of private worship, "God is eminently honored by the social worship of His people; and He delights to honor the ordinances of His public worship, by making them means of grace. Christians ought, therefore, to put a high value upon the public worship of God..."[120]

1. The opposition argues that Deuteronomy 12:32 cannot be used to support the regulative principle, for it is exclusively concerned with Old Testament tabernacle/temple worship.[121]

2. Those who use the Westminster Confession phrase about "circumstances of worship" have been answered.[122]

3. The argument that Jesus approved and participated in human traditions in synagogue worship has been partially answered.[123]

One of the most successful arguments against the regulative principle relates to the Jewish synagogues of Jesus' day. Synagogues were places of local congregational worship and education in the Law of God. The worship was not ornate and ceremonial in nature, as were the services of the temple. Synagogue worship was simple: the reading and exposition of the Law of God, prayer, and the singing of God's praises. "The synagogue...was just in name and reality the congregation of Israel localized."[124] For the formation of a local congregation that would gather for worship and instruction, i.e., a "synagogue," ten mature Jewish men had to devote their time to synagogue worship and administration. "That ten constituted a congregation was derived from [Exodus 18:21, 25; 12:4]. Similarly, it was thought to be implied in the fact, that if ten righteous men had been in Sodom, the city would not have been destroyed."[125]

Before we endeavor to answer the objection to our regulative principle that is based on the synagogue, we note that our contemporary critics are not the first to relate the synagogue to Christian worship. For centuries, Presbyterian adherents to the regulative principle have written scholarly treatises on the synagogue as a model for the worship, government, and ministry of the Christian churches in the New Testament. Some of the most respected reformed scholars include Samuel Miller, William Cunningham, John Owen, James Bannerman, John Girardeau, Douglas Bannerman, J.B. Shearer, and G.I. Williamson. Therefore, it is interesting, to say the least, that in all their studies on the synagogue, these famous scholars found nothing in the synagogue that refuted the regulative principle in which they all believed.

The critics of the regulative principle present the following syllogism regarding synagogue worship:

1. The institution of synagogue worship and instruction was not commanded by God and therefore was unregulated by the Law of God, unlike temple worship.

2. Jesus and His apostles attended worship services in the synagogues, participated in them, and approved of them.

3. Therefore, Jesus and the apostles did not practice the regulative principle of worship, for if they did they most certainly would not have participated in synagogue worship, but, rather, would have condemned it.

4. One who has used this objection against the regulative principle said confidently: "The very existence of the synagogue... undoes the regulativist's position."[126] Let us see if that is the case.

First, Jesus made His view of human traditions, not commanded by God in the worship of God, unmistakably clear. Quoting Isaiah 29:13, He says, "In vain do they worship Me, teaching as doctrines the precepts of men. Neglecting the commandment of God, you hold to the tradition of men...You are experts at setting aside the commandment of God in order to keep your tradition...thus invalidating the word of God by your tradition which you have handed down...That which proceeds out of the man, that is what defiles the man" (Mark 7:7–9, 13, 20). Therefore, any claim that Jesus accepted or participated in human traditions in the worship of God must be rejected as false, because Jesus would not contradict in His behavior what He had taught as truth from God. It would have been sinful for Jesus to participate in a form of worship not commanded by God.

Second, it is incorrect to say that the synagogue, in its institution and worship, was not regulated by the Word of God in terms of Deuteronomy 12:32, "Whatever I command you, you shall be careful to do; you shall not add to nor take away from it." We have already established that this command, rather than being exclusively tied to temple worship, as our critics allege, regulated all worship of God throughout the nation. The context of Deuteronomy 12:32 indicates this to be the case. Furthermore, Jesus and Paul both applied the regulative principle to all worship in the Christian era in Matthew 15, Mark 7, John 4 and Colossians 2.[127]

If the regulative principle states that only what is expressly and verbally commanded in the Bible may be done in worship, as our critics wrongly maintain, then their objection concerning the synagogue might have some weight. However, we have seen that this narrow interpretation of the regulative principle is not what the Bible or the *Westminster Confession of Faith* teaches. What God prescribes in the Bible for worship is found in express commands, approved examples, and necessary inferences.[128]

They seem to be arguing against a straw man. Brian Schwertley again rightly observes: "The fact that Jesus Christ participated in synagogue worship without the slightest hint of disapprobation is warrant enough."[129]

Furthermore, several passages can be brought forward from the Old Testament from which the origin and nature of synagogue worship can be honestly deduced.

> "For six days work may be done, but on the seventh day
> there is a Sabbath of complete rest, a holy convocation. You

shall not do any work; it is the Sabbath to the Lord in all
your dwellings." (Leviticus 23:3)

The weekly Sabbath is to be a day for solemn rest and holy
convocation throughout the entire nation. A holy convocation
is a gathering together and assembling of families for the
worship of God. The basic idea of "synagogue" is rooted here,
for the Greek verb form of "synagogue" means "to gather
together." It is used in Hebrews 10:25, "Not forsaking our own
assembling together..." Matthew Henry's comment on this
phrase is to the point: "It is a holy convocation, that is, 'If it lie
within your reach, you shall sanctify it in a religious assembly:
let as many as can come to the door of the tabernacle, and let
others meet elsewhere for prayer, praise, and the reading of the
Law,' as in the schools of the prophets, while prophecy
continued, and afterwards in the synagogues. Christ appointed
the New Testament Sabbath to be a holy convocation, by
meeting His disciples once and again . . . on the first day of the
week . . . Now, God's Sabbaths are to be religiously observed in
every private house, by every family apart, as well as by man
families together in holy convocations, [as indicated in Exodus
12:1–4]."[130]

*"They said in their heart, 'Let us completely subdue them.' They
have burned all the meeting places of God in the land"* (Psalm 74:8).
This psalm probably has as its reference point the invasion,
conquest, and devastation of the southern kingdom of Judah by
Nebuchadnezzar and the Babylonians in 586 B.C. All the
meeting places of God in the land were burned up along with
the temple in Jerusalem. The temple was called the "Tent of
Meeting" because it was there preeminently when Jehovah met
and fellowshipped with His holy nation. These meeting places
of God in the land were places in various localities where God
met with His people around His Word, which is the only basis
of fellowship between God and man. Acts 15:21 tells us what
occurred at these "meeting places" or "gathering places." "For
Moses from ancient generations has in every city those who
preach him, since he is read in the synagogues every Sabbath."
Such "meeting places" or "synagogues" were scattered
throughout the land, as our text indicates.

Matthew Poole says that these meeting places of God were "all the synagogues of God in the land, i.e., all the public places wherein the Jews used to meet together to worship God every Sabbath, as is noted in Acts 13:27, and upon other occasions. That the Jews had synagogues is manifest, both from these and other places of Scripture...it is undeniable that they did worship God publicly, on every Sabbath, and other holy times, even when they neither did nor could go up to Jerusalem."[131]

"Then teach them the statutes and the laws, and make known to them the way in which they are to walk and the work they are to do" *(Exodus 18:20).* R.J. Rushdoony writes of this verse: "The biblical mandate for the synagogue was found in Exodus 18:20...The synagogue was not only a place of worship but also an elementary school. The synagogue was also regarded as a kind of adult school; it was a place of lectures, and also the scene of legal decision."[132]

"Let them extol Him also in the congregation of the people, and praise Him at the seat of the elders" *(Psalm 107:32).* Douglas Bannerman, a Scottish reformed scholar of the nineteenth century, who wrote extensively on the synagogue institution, applies Psalm 107:32 to the organization of the synagogue. He writes: "The two things conjoined by the author of one of the later Psalms always went together in the synagogue system, 'the assembly of the people' and 'the seat of elders.'"[133] His point is that "the whole authority of the synagogue in every normal instance was in the hands of a small body or consistory of elders."[134]

Since the weekly Sabbath was a day of local convocations, we can deduce weekly and local synagogue worship services from the Bible, even during the days of Moses, in addition to the ceremonial worship services at the tabernacle/temple.[135] Some of the elements of worship performed in theses services also can be deduced from the Bible: the reading and exposition of the Word of God, (cf. Neh. 8:7–8; Lev. 10:8–11; Deut. 17:8–13; 24:8; 31:9–13; 33:8; 2 Chron. 15:3; 17:7–9; 19:8–10; 30:22; 35:3; Ezra 7:1–11; Ezek. 44:15, 23–24; Hosea 4:6; Mal. 2:1, 5-8; Matt. 4:23; 9:35; 13:54; Mark 1:21, 29; 6:2; Luke. 4:15–22, 44;

13:10; Acts 15:21, etc), prayer, (2 Chron. 6:34–39; Neh. 8:6; Isa. 56:7), and the singing of praises to God, (Matt. 26:30; Acts 16:25; 1 Cor. 14:26; Eph. 5:19; Col. 3:16; Heb. 13:5, and James 5:13). Virtually all regulativists recognize that the Christian church was the natural outgrowth of the synagogue, in which the covenant people conducted weekly, non-ceremonial public worship.[136] As Alfred Edersheim said, "the synagogue became the cradle of the church."[137]

The critics of the regulative principle make a serious mistake when they draw "a total antithesis between Temple worship and synagogue/Christian public worship."[138] They draw the antithesis by contrasting the ceremonial and "typical" worship of the tabernacle/temple regulated by Deuteronomy 12:32 and fulfilled in Christ with the non-ceremonial and non-typical worship services of the synagogues unregulated by Deuteronomy 12:32.

The tabernacle/temple did in fact "typify" Christ, but it was also the central place of worship for the Old Testament church (John 4:21, Matt. 21:13). It was a house of prayer, praise, and instruction. Therefore, temple worship had a greater impact on synagogue and Christian worship than is often recognized or admitted. In the New Testament, the Christian church is called a Christian "synagogue" in James 2:2; but it is also called a Christian "temple" in Ephesians 2:21 and elsewhere. The nature, worship, and purpose of the Christian church were shaped by both Old Testament institutions: the temple and the synagogue. On this subject, Michael Bushnell has made these helpful comments:

> To the OT Jew, the Temple ritual was the very epitome of worship, and all exercises of piety were in one way or another related back to that source. Liturgical practices in the synagogue in many instances corresponded directly to those of the Temple. Prayer, for example, was offered in the synagogue at the time of the Temple offerings. Outside, the Temple prayer was always offered facing the Temple or Jerusalem. The synagogues were considered sanctuaries in miniature, even to the point that the furniture in the synagogue (such as the ark and the seven-branched

candelabra) was patterned after that of the Temple.[139] Considering, therefore, the importance of the Temple even for worship outside of Jerusalem, it would seem reasonable to postulate a greater degree of continuity between Christian worship practice and certain aspects of the Temple liturgy than most authorities are willing to admit. The paucity [scarcity] of references in the literature to the influence of the Temple liturgy on Christian worship is an unbalanced situation that needs very much to be corrected. It is our opinion that the Temple rather than the synagogue is the ultimate source of a number of the most important aspects of Christian worship. That many of these aspects may have been mediated by the synagogue is beside the point, at least in so far as our concern with the subject goes.[140]

In conclusion, the critics of the regulative principle that use the synagogue argument to refute our principle make another serious mistake in presuming that the Jewish synagogue was not to be governed by Deuteronomy 12:32. They mistakenly presume that, "since there is not a set of inscripturated divine imperatives regarding the synagogue meetings, therefore what occurred in the synagogue was left to the discretion of the people...Their assumption, however, contradicts the clear teaching of the Bible. Time and again, in Old Testament and New Testament, it unequivocally condemns adding to God's Law in ethics or worship ...Human beings have no autonomy in determining the content of theology, ethics, church government or worship. Christ and His apostle Paul condemned all human traditions in worship."[141]

Closely related to the synagogue argument is the assertion of our critics that Jesus approved of and participated in Jewish religious ceremonies in worship that were never commanded by God: Seder and Chanukah. Therefore, they say, He did not practice the regulative principle of worship. This means that Christians today are free to bring whatever innovations to worship they desire, without being required to find a biblical warrant for them, as long as none of their innovations directly contradict any biblical doctrines.

First, we will consider their Seder argument. This word refers to those ancient Jewish rituals originated by the rabbis but not commanded in the Old Testament. They were invented to embellish the Passover celebration, which was commanded by God and fulfilled in the New Testament in the Lord's Supper. Seder is based on the Jewish Mishnah, which is a compilation of rabbinical oral traditions from 200 B.C. to A.D. 200. Alfred Edersheim, a leading Christian scholar on Judaism, pointed out that these rituals in the Mishnah were largely the theories and speculations of the Jewish rabbis at the end of the second century A.D. and are not the actual practice of any given period. Edersheim said: "Several of their regulations deal accordingly with obsolete customs, and have little regard to the actual circumstances of the time."[142]

The argument of our critics is that Jesus celebrated the Passover, not only in accordance with what was commanded of God, but also according to the rabbinical traditions not found in the Word of God. Therefore, they argue, Jesus did not believe that in worship, what is not commanded is forbidden, because He participated in what was not commanded, i.e., Seder.

What is the evidence our critics set forth to prove that Jesus participated in the Seder? Answer: the fact that the Bible says that during the Passover celebration, while at a meal with His disciples, Jesus drank wine. That's it! They offer no other evidence, only that at the Last Supper recorded in the Gospels, Jesus drank wine with the disciples. The fact of the matter is that *not one* of the rabbinical additions of the Seder is ever mentioned in any of the biblical accounts of the Last Supper.[143]

It was common practice among the Jews in Jesus' day to drink wine with their meals. It cannot be inferred from this fact that, because Jesus did the ordinary thing of drinking wine with his meal, he was participating in Seder. That is pure speculation with no biblical basis. Schwertley effectively answers this argument:

When the virtually universal practice of the Jews in Jesus'
day was to drink wine with their meals, is the Jewish Seder,
(which may have included among many other rituals, the
drinking of wine[144]), theory a necessary inference from the
text or pure speculation? Is it theologically and pastorally
responsible to develop a theology of worship on pure
speculation and guesswork?

But what about the use of wine? Some argue that since the
use of wine is not commanded in the original institution of
the Passover it therefore is a human innovation in a religious
ritual. Is the use of wine a violation of the regulative
principle? No, for the Passover was a meal, and the drinking
of a beverage is an ordinary, necessary circumstance of eating
(especially if one is eating roasted lamb, unleavened bread
and bitter herbs). During the feast of unleavened bread the
Israelites were commanded to eat unleavened bread for seven
days (Exodus 12:15f). Yet nothing is mentioned whatsoever
of any beverages to be drunk. Obviously God was not
requiring the Jews to die of thirst in the hot Egyptian
climate. The fact that Christ and the disciples drank wine
with (or after) their meal was not significant at all until Jesus
made it a gospel ordinance in the Lord's Supper. An
argument from an historical account must be based on the
written account itself, not on assumptions about what
happened.

Not only is the 'Jewish Seder' theory totally speculative, but
it also violates standard Protestant methods of
interpretations (i.e., the analogy of Scripture). Whenever an
interpreter encounters a difficult or unclear passage, he must
use the clearer portions of Scripture to interpret the less
clear. Does it make sense to interpret Jesus' actions at the
Last Supper in a manner that contradicts the clear teaching
of both the Old and New Testaments?...Would our Lord
participate in the Jewish Seder which included ritual hand
washings after He condemned the Pharisees in the strongest
of terms for the exact same behavior?" (emphasis original)[145]

Our critics also tell us that Jesus celebrated the Jewish
religious festival of Chanukah, which was another invention of
the rabbis, and which was not commanded by God in the Bible.
Chanukah was a Jewish festival of rabbinical tradition that

commemorated the victory of the Maccabees over the Syrians in 165 B.C., and the rededication of the temple in Jerusalem.

What is the proof our critics bring forward that Jesus participated in Chanukah? Only this: Jesus was (allegedly) present at the celebration of Chanukah, or the Feast of Dedication, according to John 10:22–23. "At that time the Feast of Dedication took place at Jerusalem; it was winter, and Jesus was walking in the Temple in the portico of Solomon." That's it! This is their proof! But this text says absolutely nothing about Jesus approving or participating in any human traditions in worship. In fact, it is not even stated that He was in Jerusalem to celebrate the Feast of Dedication or Chanukah. All the text says is that Jesus was in Jerusalem during the time of its celebration. There is not even a shred of evidence in the Bible that Jesus celebrated Chanukah.

In the seventeenth century, Scottish Presbyterian George Gillespie, who was a commissioner to the Westminster Assembly, completely refuted this theory imposed on John 10:22–23.

> We must remember, that the circumstances only of time and place are noted by the evangelist, for evidence to the story, and not for any mystery. Christ had come up to the feast of tabernacles (John 7), and tarried still all that while, because then there was a great confluence of people in Jerusalem. Whereupon He took occasion to spread the net of the gospel for catching many souls. And whilst John says, "It was at Jerusalem the feast of the dedication," he gives a reason only of the confluence of many people at Jerusalem, and shows how it came to pass that Christ had occasions to preach to such a multitude; and whilst he adds, "and it was winter," he gives reason of Christ's walking in Solomon's porch, whither the Jews resort was. It was not thought beseeming to walk in the temple itself, but in the porch men used to convene either for talking or walking, because in the summer the porch shadowed them from the heat. Others think, that whilst he says, it was winter, imports that therefore Christ was the more frequently in the temple, knowing that His time was short which He had then for His preaching; for in the entry of the next spring He was to suffer.[146]

Thus, this use of speculation in interpreting the Bible to "overthrow the many clear passages of Scripture which unequivocally condemn human traditions in the religious sphere [must be rejected as false]. Such a procedure is nothing more than self-deception, excuse making and a grasping after straw."[147]

Some of our critics claim that when Jesus read from Isaiah in the synagogue in Nazareth, recorded in Luke 4:16-21, He was "violating" the regulative principle. What? The reading and preaching of the Word of God in worship is clearly inferred from the Bible. The critic uses Deuteronomy 30:9-13 to support his view. It commands God's Law to be read every seven years at the feast of the tabernacles to the whole gathered nation, but that passage is not even concerned with synagogue worship. Furthermore, the entire Old Testament is referred to by the New Testament as "Law" (John 10:34; Rom. 3:19). For example, in 1 Corinthians 14:21, the apostle writes, "In the Law it is written," and then he quotes Isaiah 28:11-12. If our critic "was fair to his opponents and used a correct interpretation of the regulative principle, he would not offer up such ludicrous argument."[148]

Our critics also argue that the apostle Paul allowed the first generation of Jewish Christians to continue to practice certain Jewish ceremonies. True. However, this fact cannot be used to disprove the regulative principle, for several reasons. (1) These ceremonies were not man-made traditions or rabbinical traditions; they originated with the Old Testament revelation from God. These ceremonies could not be forced upon non-Jewish Christians (Rom. 14:5f). They were allowed because of the unique historical situation. "The first generation of Christians lived in a period in which the old order was coming to an end. Christ brought to an end all the ceremonial aspects of the Law when He died on the cross (e.g., animal sacrifices, Jewish holy days, circumcision, etc.). Yet prior to the end of the age when the Jews were divorced and judged as a nation and the temple was destroyed (A.D. 70), God allowed a period of transition. If [our critic] wishes to argue that modern Jewish believers should continue keeping certain ceremonial laws, perhaps he could explain why that which is anticipatory, typical, and thus temporary, should continue. That which the Bible calls the inferior, Hebrews 9:11-15, the shadow, Hebrews 10:1; 8:4-5, the obsolete, Hebrews 8:13, the symbolic, Hebrews 9:9, and the ineffectual, Hebrews 10:4, does not continue."[149]

Another popular argument among critics of the regulative principle is based on the Feast of Purim in Esther 9:20–22, "Then Mordecai recorded these events, and he sent letters to all the Jews who were in all the provinces of King Ahasuerus, both near and far, obliging them to celebrate the fourteenth day of the month Adar, and the fifteenth day of the same month annually, because on those days the Jews rid themselves of their enemies, and it was a month which was turned for them from sorrow into gladness and from mourning into a holiday [lit., a good day], that they should make them days of feasting and rejoicing and sending portions of food to one another and gifts to the poor."

They present their case in the following way: The Feast of Purim ordered by Mordecai in Esther 9:20–22 is an example of how the Jews instituted a new feast and holy day without any command from God, and therefore, they say that Christians can institute new religious rituals and holy days without any command from God in the Bible. This argument is so flawed that it can be easily rejected.

First, although the NASV uses the word "holiday" in its translation of verse 22, a more literal and accurate translation would be "a good day." The text is clear that this was not the institution of another Sabbath or holy day; rather it was the institution of a day of thanksgiving. No mention is made of religious rituals or worship services to be performed on that day. The *Westminster Confession of Faith* takes Esther 9:20–22 as its Scriptural support for occasional days of thanksgiving, or to use its words, for "thanksgivings upon special occasions."[150] Our reformed fathers saw no contradiction, therefore, between their statement on "thanksgivings upon special occasions" and their statement: *"There is no day commanded in Scripture to be kept holy under the gospel but the Lord's day, which is the Christian Sabbath. Festival days, vulgarly called* "Holy-days," having no warrant in the Word of God, are not to be continued. Nevertheless, it is lawful and necessary, upon special emergent occasions, to separate a day or days for public fasting or thanksgiving, as the several eminent and extraordinary dispensations of God's providence shall administer cause and opportunity to His people" (Appendix to *Westminster's Directory for the Public Worship of God*).

Second, The Feast of Purim was not instituted by the leaders of the church as a holy day, but rather "it came about because of a unique historical event in Israel's salvation history. The festival was decreed by the civil magistrate (the prime minister, Mordecai, and the queen, Esther). Religious leaders had nothing to do with it. After the civil decree, it was agreed to unanimously by the people."[151]

Third, the argument that Purim proves that we are allowed to create new rites and holy days cannot be true, for if it were, it would contradict what the Bible says clearly elsewhere in Deuteronomy 4:2; 12:32; Proverbs 30:5, etc.

God often calls His people by His providence to times of fasting and times of thanksgiving; it is our duty to comply and to set apart time to do either as the occasion dictates. But this is totally different from establishing regularly recurring holy days, i.e., Sabbaths. In times of thanksgiving for special favor and deliverances from God, a day is chosen for the duty of giving thanks. But when a holy day is instituted, what is done on that day is determined by the sanctity of the day. For example, the alleged sanctity of December 25 determines what we should do on that day. Holy days, created by the church calendar, e.g., Christmas, Easter, Good Friday, Lent, and the like "interfere with the free use of that time which the Creator has granted to man; detract from the honor due to the day of sacred rest which He has appointed; lead to impositions over conscience; have been the...source of superstition and idolatry; and have been productive of the worse effects upon morals, in every age, and among every people, barbarous and civilized, pagan and

Christian, popish and protestant, among whom they have been observed."[152]

For all these reasons, any holy days invented by man, in addition to the weekly Sabbath, and all human traditions in the worship of God, have been rejected by the Reformed Presbyterian Church in the United States, which allows no stated religious days but the Christian Sabbath.[153]

CHAPTER SEVEN

POPULAR INNOVATIONS TO WORSHIP

THE USE OF PRESCRIBED LITURGIES IN PUBIC WORSHIP

Many helpful critiques of prescribed liturgies in public worship have been written through the years. They include:

- George Gillespie, *The English Popish Ceremonies*, originally written in the mid-sixteen hundreds, recently reprinted by Naphtali Press, P.O. Box 141084, Dallas, TX 75214;

- Westminster divines, including Samuel Rutherford, *The Divine Right of Church Government*, reprinted by Napthali Press;

- Thomas M'Crie, "On the English Liturgy," pages 205 and following in his *Miscellaneous Writings* (1841);

- James Bannerman, *The Church of Christ*, Vol. I, pages. 322–421, originally printed in 1896, reprinted by Still Waters Revival Books, 12810-126 St. Edmonton, AB, Canada T5L 0Y1);

- Robert L. Dabney, "The 'Tabernacle' and the 'Abbey,'" pages 32 and following in his *Discussions*, Vol.

V, published by Sprinkle Publications, Harrisonburg, VA;

- John Owen, "A Discourse Concerning Liturgies," page 397 in his *Works*, Vol. XIX, (1826 edition), first published in the mid-sixteen hundreds, recently reprinted by The Banner of Truth Trust, Edinburgh, Scotland;

- Samuel Miller, *Presbyterianism: The Truly Primitive and Apostolical Constitution of the Church of Christ*, (published in 1835), page 68.

Prescribed Liturgies means the required and precise reading and pronouncing of the words set down in a liturgical book read "without alteration, diminution or addition."[154] And the issue is this: "Is it lawful and expedient to have set forms of prayers for every part of the public service of God, the use of which shall be authoritatively *imposed* upon all the ministers of the Church, and which they shall be bound to *repeat invariably* on the same day of every recurring year, without the slightest diminution, addition, or alteration?"[155]

In order to understand the issue of prescribed liturgies, we must understand what the issue is *not*. (1) It is not about the lawfulness of ever using in worship "studied" prayers, i.e., well-prepared, thought-out, and orderly prayers, sometimes even written down word-for-word. Prayers in public worship should be well prepared and thought-out beforehand. They should be "premeditated and pre-composed" by whomever is leading the worship service.

In opposing prescribed liturgies, we are not arguing that all prayers must be extemporaneous and unplanned. If the minister plans what he will say to the congregation in his sermon, then surely he will plan what he will say as he leads the congregation in prayer to Almighty God. (2) Nor are we arguing against prayers that are written by others, as long as they are reverently written and thoroughly biblical in content. And, (3) we are not arguing against praying the Lord's Prayer verbatim in worship.

As the *Westminster Larger Catechism* Q. 187 says: "The Lord's prayer is not only for direction, as a pattern, according to which we are to make other prayers; but may also be used as a prayer, so that it be done with understanding, faith, reverence, and other graces necessary to the right performance of the duty of prayer."

The issue is this: What is "the lawfulness of liturgies in the strict sense of the word, or of fixed forms of prayer, imposed by ecclesiastical authority in the stated and ordinary worship of God. There are three elements included in the notion of such human impositions in the ordinary worship of God. First, we have a scheme of pre-composed and fixed forms of prayer for the ordinary worship of the Church at all times. Second, we have these used alone, and to the exclusion of the possibility of free and extempore prayer. And third, we have the stated use of liturgies, to the exclusion of other forms of prayer, imposed as binding by ecclesiastical authority, under the penalty of forfeiting, by declinature of them, the privilege of Church fellowship. These three things are included in the notion of a prescribed liturgy as statedly used in the Church. The stated and universal use of such forms of prayer, the exclusion as unlawful of any other, and the imposition of them by ecclesiastical authority are properly implied in the principle of liturgies prescribed by the Church."[156]

Neither the Old Testament nor the New Testament contain the slightest hint that the church is obligated to use set forms of prayer as in a prescribed liturgy to the exclusion of every other kind of prayer, including those extemporaneously uttered. Matthew and Luke do not even use the same words in recording the Lord's Prayer. Hence, including them as a necessary element in the worship of God is going beyond what God has commanded. They do not have the slightest warrant in Scripture. They form no part of the worship itself, not being sanctioned by the authority of Christ in His Word.

Some try to justify prescribed liturgies, not as acts of worship, but as necessary "circumstances" of worship without which the worship service could not be performed with propriety, decency, and in an orderly fashion as commanded by God. They us the statement of Paul, "All things must be done properly and in an orderly manner" (1 Cor. 14:40).[157]

Nineteenth century Presbyterian Samuel Miller has documented that "no prescribed liturgies were used in the apostolic age of the Church...No such thing as a prescribed form of prayer appears to have been known in the Christian Church for several hundred years after Christ"[158] But what about the alleged liturgies of St. Mark, St. James and the like? Research has shown them all to be forgeries. What about the liturgies attributed to Chrysostom, Basil, and other early church fathers? "Bishop White, an English prelate, who lived in the seventeenth century, delivers the following opinion: 'The Liturgies fathered upon St. Basil and St. Chrysostom, have a known mother, (to wit, the Church of Rome); but there is (besides many other just exceptions) so great a dissimilitude between the supposed fathers of their children, that they rather argue the dishonest dealings of their mother, than serve as lawful witnesses of that which the adversary intended to prove by them.'"[159]

> "If the Apostles, or any apostolic men, had prepared and given to the Church anything like a Liturgy, we should, doubtless, have had it preserved, and transmitted with care to posterity. The Church, in this case, would have had one uniform book of prayers, which would have been in use, and held precious, throughout the whole Christian community. But nothing of this kind has ever been pretended to exist...Accordingly, when Liturgies were gradually introduced into general use, in the sixth and subsequent centuries, on account of the decline of piety and learning among the clergy, there was no uniformity even among the churches of the same state or kingdom."[160]

> Confining ministers to forms of prayer in public worship tends to restrain and discourage the spirit of prayer. We cannot help thinking that the constant repetition of the same words, from year to year, tends to produce, at least with many persons, dullness and a loss of interest. A constant form is a certain way to bring the soul to a cold, insensible, formal worship. (Richard Baxter)[161]

It is no small argument against confining ministers and people to a prescribed form, that whenever religion is in a lively state in the heart of the minister accustomed to use a liturgy, and especially when it is powerfully revived among the members of his church, his form of prayer will seldom fail to be deemed an undesirable restraint; and this feeling will commonly either vent itself in fervent extemporary prayer, or result in languor and decline under restriction to his form. The more rigorous and exclusive the confinement to a prescribed form, the more cold and lifeless will the prevailing formality generally be found. (Samuel Miller)[162]

A frequent argument in favor of prescribed liturgies is that the Scottish Church had an order of worship produced by John Knox based on forms of worship used in Strasbourg, Frankfort, and Geneva written by John Calvin, William Farel, and others. In 1564 the General Assembly enacted that "everie minister, exhorter, and reader shall have one of the Psalme Bookes latelie printed in Edinburgh, and use the Order contained therein in prayers, marriage, and ministration of Sacraments."

Scholars differ as to the exact character and authority of this order of worship. Someone has referred to it as "the National Prayer Book," and "the authorized liturgy of the Scottish Church." However, many reformed historians of the Scottish Church have another opinion. One scholar, alluding to Knox's own words in *Works*, Vol. VI, page 281, says that it was not a prescribed form but "a guide and directory." Another held that "even the form, such as it was, partook more of the character of a directory than of a liturgy, and that the minister was not restricted to the words of the book."[163] Others believe that it was no more than a guide or model, "far less observed as a rigid liturgy."[164] A more complete interpretation is that of a leading historian, J. King Hewison:

The [Scottish] Confession repudiates all constitutions and articles invented by men and not "expressed in His Word," while it declares that "any Policy and any Order in Ceremonies...are both temporal." The Book of Discipline, although it does not mention in this connection the Liturgy, condemns "as damnable to man's salvation" any imposition upon the consciences of men, which is not expressly commanded in Scripture. The Liturgy rested upon no "express Commandment." Knox, who believed that the English Prayer Book was a device "for upholding of massing priests," and "any jot whereof will I never counsel any man to use," could not consistently authorize the book for any other purpose than as a guide. The Book of Discipline itself states the object of the Order, it being "sufficient to instruct the diligent reader," i.e., not merely the church reader, but any reader. The function of the public reader was to read the Common Prayers in church and to teach children by means of that lesson-book. When the Book of Discipline indicates what is necessary to retain the church in good order, it includes "Common prayers publicly made"...not read; and, in the next paragraph, the danger of oft-repeating "the Common Prayers," that is, out of the Order, is pointed out thus: "What day the public sermon is, we can neither require nor greatly approve that the Common Prayers be publicly used, lest that we should either foster the people in superstition, who come to prayers as they come to the masse.

The continuous and imperative use of a liturgy was unharmonious with the spirit of the Reformers, who relied upon the inspiration of the Holy Spirit in prayer. The half-educated substitutes for ministers did require such mental crutches, as the Book of Discipline admitted, "'till they grow to greater perfection." The intention of the manual was conformity of practice, but not literal conformity. Alexander Henderson of Leuchars, in his Order and Government of the Church of Scotland, refers to the Form of Prayers as that "to which ministers are to conform themselves, . . . although they be not tied to set forms and words, yet are they not left at random, but, for testifying their consent and keeping unity, they have their directory and prescribed order." In similar terms, the well-informed Calderwood the historian states: "none are tied to the prayers of that book; but the prayers are set down as samplers." Still more convincing is his testimony in his famous Altare Damascenum to this effect: "We also, it is true, have in our Church 'Agenda' and an order to be kept in sacred services; but no one is bound to the prayers or exhortations of our liturgy. They are set forth only as models by which the contents and the forms of prayers or exhortations are as to substantials pointed out, but not that the ministers should be tied to the very words.

Never in the thirteen years of my ministry have I, either in the observance of sacraments or other sacred offices, made use of the exhortations or prayers contained in our 'Agenda.' The same has been the case with very many others, and it is free even to every one to do likewise. Moreover, as it seems to me, it is childish to do otherwise."[165]

THE ADDITION OF HOLY DAYS
IN THE CHURCH CALENDAR

The *Westminster Directory of Public Worship* (appendix) states: "There is no day commanded in Scripture to be kept holy under the Gospel but the Lord's Day, which is the Christian Sabbath. Festival days, vulgarly called 'Holy-days,' having no warrant in the Word of God, are not to be continued." If the church is free to create holy days, as some of the critics of the regulative principle assert, then why was the Lord angry with King Jeroboam for having instituted a feast in the eighth month on the fifteenth day of the month...which he had devised in his own heart? (1 Kings 12:32–33).

Samuel Miller of Princeton Seminary, in his book, *Presbyterianism: The Truly Primitive and Apostolical Constitutions of the Church of Christ*, (1835), wrote: "The observance of uncommanded holy-days is ever found to interfere with the due sanctification of the Lord's Day. Adding to the appointments of God is superstition. And superstition has ever been found unfriendly to genuine obedience...there is, perhaps, no fact more universal and unquestionable that that the zealous observers of stated fasts and festivals are characteristically lax in the observance of that one day which God has eminently set apart for himself, and on the sanctification of which all the vital interests of practical religion are suspended."

John Dick of Scotland in his *Lectures in Theology* (1836) writes: "Thus [Sunday] is the only day which God claims as His own in a peculiar sense; He has given us the other six days to pursue our secular employments. It follows, that men have no right to institute holidays, which return as regularly at certain intervals as the Sabbath does at the beginning of the week. This is an assumption of authority which God has not delegated to them. Holidays are an encroachment upon the time of which He has made a free gift to men for their worldly affairs; and although enforced by civil and ecclesiastical laws, they are not binding upon the conscience. No man sins in not observing them; but he does sin, if he observes them from an opinion of their holiness. Men may set apart particular days for fasting and thanksgiving; but those are only occasional, and not the days, but the services, are holy."

The General Assembly of the Presbyterian Church in the United States in 1899 declared: "There is no warrant in Scripture for the observance of Christmas and Easter as holy days, rather the contrary, Galatians 4:9–11; Colossians 2:16–21, and such observance is contrary to the principles of the reformed faith, conducive to will-worship, and not in harmony with the simplicity of the Gospel of Jesus Christ."

Morton Smith of Greenville Presbyterian Theological Seminary in his book, *How is the Gold Become Dim* (1973) wrote: "It is just this attitude of indifference to the Constitution (Westminster Standards) that has brought us to the state we are in the P.C.U.S. Whereas, earlier, as is reflected in the 1899 deliverance about Christmas and Easter, there was meticulous concern for staying with the standards, and the strict interpretation of Scripture on even such a matter as these two days. Now there is complete reversal to the point of adopting the liturgical calendar of past tradition, without any biblical basis." In other words, once the regulative principle of worship is cast aside by a church, that church is on a slippery slope to apostasy.

THE USE OF VESTMENTS
BY THE MINISTER IN WORSHIP

John a Lasco (1548) was a great Polish Reformer and preacher of the gospel. He wrote a helpful article against the wearing of vestments, surplices, clerical collars, and other clerical garb by the minister leading public worship.[166] It is reprinted in *The Reformation of the Church*, edited by Iain

Murray, published by The Banner of Truth Trust in 1965. His arguments are as follows.

> The things which ought definitely to be kept out of the church are twofold: (1) Certain things that are so obviously impious that they can never deceive even those who are but little instructed in the Word of God, such as the worship of images, adoration of the bread and wine, profanation of the Lord's Supper by the mass . . . prayer for the dead, and innumerable similar monstrosities which Antichrist (the papacy) has brought into Christ's Church. There are other things, (2) Introduced by the same Antichrist, which contend strongly with Christian liberty, obscure Christ, increase hypocrisy and bring pride into the Church. At the same time, however, they bear upon them the appearance of utility and splendor. Of this sort are appointed fast days, limitation of foods, much singing which is not understood in the Church [because in Latin] . . . and the use of vestments in the administration of the Lord's Supper. There is not now the space to record how much harm has crept into the Church from these individual things, and how much more could creep in if they are not abolished; I can here only treat of the use of vestments, because they must by no means be tolerated any longer in the reformed Church of Christ by a pious teacher.

> 1. By means of the argument by which Christ and the prophets together with the apostles expel from the Church human dogmas and inventions as a plague, Mat. 12, Isa. 29, Col. 2, I too am convinced that vestments are a human invention which ought to be removed from the Church.

> 2. Those who wish to retain the use of vestments in the Church . . . refer to the priesthood of Aaron. But let them take a little care of what they are saying, for according to the Scriptures Christ is a priest according to the order not of Aaron but of Melchizedek, and the priesthood of Aaron has in Christ been abolished, together with all its parts, among which we number vestments, [such as the High Priest's uniform]. And thus Christ . . . did not use in divine service any new or special kind of vestments or prescribe their use, for the

foreshadowing priesthood was done away with by the true priest Christ...Now it is clear that teaching and commandment of a special kind of vestments in God's ministry is a transgression of the divine law because the Aaronic priesthood is thus recalled" (p. 65).

3. Paul simply admitted nothing into the Church unless it edified, that is, increased godliness. Special vestments in the ministry do not edify but destroy; they are therefore not to be tolerated. Nor do those things edify which provide an imaginary occasion for piety, but they must provide Christians with a compelling opportunity for piety. But vestments, on the contrary, sometimes increase pride in those who use them, sometimes hypocrisy, sometimes both. It is very easy for them to provide an opportunity for hypocrisy, indeed it is unavoidable; if there is really in oneself that virtue which you imagine to be signified in vestments, why do you receive a reward from men by declaring it? But there is not, and the hypocrite in you is shown up, who are a different man from what you appear to be (p. 66).

4. Moreover, there is danger that a reputation of merit or some such foolish thing should be occasioned by the idea that the dignity of the ministers or the sacraments or the preaching of the Word is violated unless it is supplied with this useless and pernicious clothing. This fear alone of human merit should move us to exclude from the temple vestments together with the other ceremonies introduced by human invention (p. 67).

5. I know that it is objected by some that sacred services are adorned by vestments. Nay, they are much obscured. For vestments assail the eyes of men and remove their minds from the contemplation of the sacred things which are taking place in the sacraments and lead them to the pleasures of the senses. Holy simplicity commends the institutions of God (p. 67).

6. Finally, since Paul commands us to beware of every kind of evil, and we have shown that to prescribe vestments in the administration of holy things is truly an evil, who will not judge that they should be avoided, for they are indeed a human invention, parts of the Aaronic or papistical priesthood, edifying nothing, but begetting pride, hypocrisy and the reputation of merit (p. 68).

7. Objection (from some): In indifferent matters the weakness of our brethren is to be considered . . . Answer: You would surely deny that those things are indifferent which obscure the priesthood of Christ, and produce from themselves nothing except hypocrisy, sects, and pride in the church, have no source in the Scriptures, and are commanded with tyranny unworthy of Christians (p. 68).

8. There is one way of safety if we altogether turn to repentance: believe the gospel of Christ, walk in innocence of life, and retain nothing in the church which does not either have the express word of God, or else take its infallible origin from that source. Then let true pastors, zealous for teaching, be set over the churches, and let dumb and wicked pastors be shut out; thus king will flourish with people, according to the promises of God (p. 69).

THE USE OF THE "ALTAR CALL" IN PUBLIC WORSHIP

The "invitational system," invented by Charles G. Finney in the early 1800s and perfected by Billy Graham in the late 1900s, should not be used in the worship of God for several reasons. First and foremost, it has no warrant in the Word of God. It is an addition to God's commands governing worship, not being commanded by God. Second, it blurs the free offer of the gospel. At the conclusion of the sermon the altar call is given and people are told to walk to the front of the sanctuary while the congregation is singing a song, if they want to be "born again," "be saved," "confess Christ," "decide for Christ," or "rededicate themselves to Christ." By doing this the practitioners of this *superstitious device* have uncritically married the free offer of the gospel and the call of faith and repentance with the "invitation" to "come forward." Third, it is misdirected and misdirecting in that it focuses on man's decision rather than on the work of the Holy Spirit. Fourth, it is infective in that, like a malaria-carrying mosquito, it carries with it doctrinal and ethical sicknesses growing in the historical soil from which it springs. Having been born in a deficient theological context (the Arminianism and perfectionism of Finney), it always brings heretical elements still clinging to it whenever it is adopted as a part of the worship service. Fifth, the altar call de-emphasizes the importance of the sacraments of baptism and the Lord's Supper, almost making itself a third sacrament. How often preachers are heard to say as they give the invitation, "Coming forward does not save you; but it *seals* your decision for Christ." Only sacraments are signs and *seals* of salvation! And sixth, it is cruel, because it leads people away from the light of God's truth. (For an explanation of these charges and a more thorough explaining of "the invitational system" from a reformed perspective, see my paper, "Why I Don't Give 'Invitations': A Discussion of the Failure of the 'Invitational System' to Uphold the Free Offer of the Gospel of Free Grace.")

THE PRACTICE OF COMING FORWARD AND KNEELING TO RECEIVE THE LORD'S SUPPER

Coming forward and kneeling to receive the Lord's Supper from the hand of the minister or priest in some Protestant churches is a "hangover" from the rituals of Roman Catholicism. This is forbidden because it is not commanded in the Word of God. It was unknown in the Christian Church for several centuries after the apostolic age. In fact, in the second, third, and fourth centuries, it was considered unlawful to kneel in worship on the Lord's Day, since kneeling was the posture of solemn fasting and not of the celebration and joy of worship in the presence of the risen Lord. Even the famous Council of Nicea (A.D. 381) forbade kneeling on the Lord's Day! Coming forward and kneeling to receive the Lord's Supper was not introduced until the doctrine of transubstantiation[167] made its appearance in the Roman Catholic Church.

The Lord's Supper is a covenant meal, and therefore its administration must resemble eating a meal. A meal is eaten at a table with one family member passing the food to the one next to him until all have food on their plates and are fellowshipping with each other around the table. The first Lord's Supper was in connection with a meal. "It is granted, on all hands, that the posture in which the Lord's Supper was first administered by the Savior Himself, was that in which it was customary to receive ordinary meals...The Evangelist Matthew declares: Now when the evening was come, He sat down with the twelve. And as they were eating, Jesus took bread and blessed it, and brake it, and gave it to His disciples."[168]

For this reason, the *Westminster Directory of Public Worship*, calls the Lord's Supper, "That heavenly feast, recommends that after this exhortation, warning, and invitation, the table being before decently covered, and so conveniently placed, that the communicants may orderly sit about it, or at it." Therefore, Samuel Miller explains: "The essential nature of the Eucharist [the Lord's Supper] renders the attendance upon it in a kneeling posture incongruous, and, of course, unsuitable. This ordinance is a feast, a feast of love, joy and thanksgiving. The very name, Eucharist, implies as much. It is intended to be a sign of love, confidence and affectionate fellowship, between each communicant and the Master of the feast, and between the members of His Body. It is also intended to be an emblem, and a means of that spiritual nourishment which is found in feeding by faith, and, in a spiritual sense, on the body and blood of the Redeemer, set forth in this ordinance as crucified for us."[169]

THE MAKING OF THE SIGN OF THE CROSS

A practice has developed through the centuries of making the sign of the cross at baptism and many other times. The first reason to reject it is that it is an addition to the Word of God concerning worship. It is not commanded by God; therefore, it has no divine warrant and is forbidden. It is a human invention. It has always been associated with superstition. "The sign of the cross was thought...a sure preservative against all sorts of malignity, poisons, or fascination, and effectual to drive away evil spirits...When we consider the miserable superstition with which the use of the sign of the cross is constantly marked by Roman Catholics; that they regard it as essential to the validity of the ordinance of baptism; that they adore it; that they apply it in every step and act of religious life...and that they rely upon it as a kind of talisman, connected with every blessing...surely, when we see this degrading system of superstition connected with this sign...acknowledged on all hands to be a mere human invention...it is no wonder that enlightened and conscientious Christians should feel constrained to lay it aside."[170]

The Practice of Bowing at the Name of Jesus

Bowing the head whenever the name Jesus is mentioned, as in the Apostles' Creed, is frequently practiced among liturgical churches, such as the Episcopal and Anglican. We reject it because it is not commanded in the Word of God. It has no divine warrant and is therefore a human invention. Although we cannot pronounce the name of Jesus our Savior with too much reverence, we may not add to the Word of God. This practice is arbitrary. Why would one bow at the name of Jesus and not at His other glorious titles, e.g., God, Redeemer, Savior, Christ, and Immanuel? "Is not the habit of such observances, without warrant, and, as would seem, without reason, plainly adapted to beget a spirit of superstition and to occupy our minds with the commandments of men, rather than with the ordinances of Heaven?"[171]

The Use of Pictures of Jesus and Other Icons in the Worship of God

"You shall not make for yourself a graven image."
(Exodus 20:4)

The following quotes against pictures and icons in the worship of God are by John Calvin, taken from the *Institutes of the Christian Religion*, I, XI, Battles edition. (This entire section in the *Institutes* should be read and studied.)

> Therefore, that exclusive definition, encountered everywhere, annihilates all the divinity that men fashion for themselves out of their own opinion: for God Himself is the sole and proper witness of Himself. Meanwhile since this brute stupidity gripped the whole world . . . to pant after visible figures of God, and thus to form gods of wood, stone, gold, silver, or other dead and corruptible matter . . . we must cling to this principle: God's glory is corrupted by an impious falsehood whenever any form is attached to Him" (p. 100).

> God's majesty is sullied by an unfitting and absurd fiction, when the incorporeal is made to resemble corporeal matter, the invisible a visible likeness, the spirit an inanimate object, the immeasurable a puny bit of wood, stone, or gold...every statue man erects, or every image he paints to represent God, simply displeases God as something dishonorable to Him (p. 101).

> I know that it is pretty much an old saw that images are the books of the uneducated...yet the Spirit of God declares otherwise...For when Jeremiah declares that the wood is a doctrine of vanity, Jeremiah 10:8; when Habakkuk teaches that a molten image is a teacher of falsehood, Habakkuk 2:18, from such statements we must surely infer this general doctrine, that whatever men learn of God from images is futile, indeed false... the prophets totally condemn the notion, taken as axiomatic by the papists, that images stand in place of books. For the prophets set images over against the true God as contraries that can never agree...when we teach that it is vanity and falsehood for men to try to fashion God in images, we are doing nothing else but repeating word for word what the prophets have taught (p. 105).

> [The Council of Elvira (a.d. 305) declared:] It is decreed that there shall be no pictures in churches, that what is reverenced or adored be not depicted on the walls (p. 106).

> Brothels show harlots clad more virtuously and modestly than the churches show those objects which they wish to be thought images of virgins (p. 107).

But then we shall also answer that this is not the method of teaching within the sacred precincts of believing folk, whom God wills to be instructed there with a far different doctrine than this trash. In the preaching of the Word and sacred mysteries He has bidden that a common doctrine be there set forth for all. But those whose eyes rove about in contemplating idols betray that their minds are not diligently intent upon this doctrine...But whence, I pray you, this stupidity if not because they are defrauded of that doctrine which alone was fit to instruct them? (p. 107).

Man's mind, full as it is of pride and boldness, dares to imagine a god according to its own capacity; as it sluggishly plods, indeed is overwhelmed with the crassest ignorance, it conceives an unreality and an empty appearance as God. To these evils a new wickedness enjoins itself, that man tries to express in his work the sort of God he has inwardly conceived. Therefore the mind begets the idol; the hand gives it birth. The example of the Israelites shows the origin of idolatry to be that men do not believe God is with them unless He shows Himself physically present. "We know not," they said, "what has become of this Moses; make us gods who may go before us," Exodus 32:1. They knew, indeed, that this was God whose power they had experienced in very many miracles; but they did not trust that He was near them unless they could discern with their eyes a physical symbol of His countenance (p. 108).

Any use of images leads to idolatry. Adoration promptly follows upon this sort of fancy: for when men thought they gazed upon God in images, they also worshipped Him in them. Finally, all men, having fixed their minds and eyes upon them, began to grow more brutish and to be overwhelmed with admiration for them, as if something of divinity inhered there...Therefore, when you prostrate yourself in veneration, representing to yourself in an image either a god or a creature, you are already ensnared in some superstition...And there is no difference whether they simply worship an idol, or God in the idol. It is always idolatry when divine honors are bestowed upon an idol, under whatever pretext this is done. And because it does not please God to be worshipped superstitiously, whatever is conferred upon the idol is snatched away from Him (p. 109).

Not content with spiritual understanding, they thought that through the images a surer and closer understanding would be impressed upon them. Once this perverse imitation of God pleased them, they never stopped until, deluded by new tricks, they presently supposed that God manifested His power in images (p. 110).

And yet I am not gripped by the superstition of thinking absolutely no images permissible. But because sculpture and painting are gifts of God, I seek a pure and legitimate use of each, lest those things which the Lord has conferred upon us for His glory and our good be not only polluted by perverse misuse but also turned to our destruction...for about five hundred years [after Christ's death and resurrection], during which religion was still flourishing, and purer doctrine thriving, Christian churches were commonly empty of images. Thus, it was when the purity of the ministry had somewhat degenerated that they were first introduced for the adornment of the churches (pp. 112–113).

The following quotes are not from Calvin, but from one of Calvin's successors at Geneva, Francis Turretin, from his book, *Institutes of Eclectic Theology*, Vol. II, pp. 62f.

Thus we do not condemn historical representations of events or of great men, either symbolical (by which their virtues and vices are represented) or political (impressed upon coins). But we here treat of sacred and religious images which are supposed to contribute something to the excitation of religious feeling.

The question is not whether it is lawful to represent creatures and to exhibit with the pencil historical events (either for the sake of ornament or for delight or even for instruction and to recall . . . past events) for this no one of us denies. Rather the question is whether it is lawful to represent God Himself and the persons of the Trinity by any image; if not by an immediate and proper similitude to set forth a perfect image of the nature of God...at least by analogy or metaphorical and mystical significations. This our adversaries maintain; we deny.

Finally, the question is not whether it is lawful to have in our houses representations of holy men for a recollection of their piety and an example for imitation. Rather the question is whether it is right to set them up in sacred places...not for worship and veneration, but for strongly impressing believers and exciting their affections by bringing up past things (which the Lutherans affirm...we deny.)

The reasons are: First, God expressly forbids this in the second commandment, where two things are prohibited—both the making of images for worship and the worshipping of them. Nor can it be replied that it [the 2nd commandment] refers only to images of false gods. Moses himself clearly explained not representing God, Deuteronomy 4:12; yea, even God Himself (the best interpreter of His own law) intimates this, Isaiah 40:18. Hence the Israelites representing God by the image of a calf were sharply rebuked and heavily punished, Exodus 32.

Second, God, being boundless...and invisible...can be represented by no image.

Third, that ought to be distant from sacred places which does not belong to the worship of God and is joined with danger to idolatry. Now images in sacred places do not belong to the worship of God, since indeed God has expressly removed them from His worship by the law and they are connected with the most imminent danger of idolatry. For men . . . are moved to the worship of them by the very reverence for the place, as experience shows...[The Lutherans object:] that only worship makes the images unlawful, from which Lutherans profess that they shrink. We answer that although they are not expressly worshipped by them (as by the papists) by bowing the knee and burning incense to them or offering prayers, still they cannot be said to be free from all worship; if not direct, at least indirect and participative because they hold that by images and the sight of them they conceive holy thoughts concerning God and Christ (which cannot but belong to the worship of God, so that thus they really worship God by images) (pp. 62–64).

The consequence does not hold good from the figures of the temple at Jerusalem to the images of Christians. The former were commanded and the latter were not; those typical and fulfilled in the New Testament, these not; the former placed almost out of sight of the people and danger of adoration, which cannot be said of the latter. Nor is Christian liberty to be brought up here (which is not the license of doing anything whatsoever in relation to the worship of God, but is the immunity from the malediction of the law and the slavery of ceremonies). Since the former figures pertained to these, they also are to be considered as equally abrogated in the New Testament (p. 66).

Therefore, as the Westminster Confession of Faith states in chapter XXI, paragraph I: "The acceptable way of worshipping the true God is instituted by Himself, and so limited by His own revealed will, that He may not be worshipped . . . under any visible representation, or any other way not prescribed in the Holy Scripture."

THE DANGEROUS CONSEQUENCES OF ADDING TO THE COMMANDS OF GOD

According to Richard Baxter in *A Christian Directory*, page 70, the following are the dangerous consequences of adding to the commands of God:

1. "They tend to dethrone Christ from His sovereignty, and legislative prerogative.

2. "And to advance man, blind and sinful man, into His place.

3. "And thereby to debase religion, making it but a human or a mixed thing (and it can be no more noble than its author is).

4. "And thereby they debase also the church of God, and the government of it, while they make it to be but a human policy, and not divine.

5. "They tend to depose God from His authority in men's consciences, and to level or join Him there but with man.

6. "They tend to men's doubtfulness and uncertainty of their religion; seeing man is fallible, and so may his constitutions be.

7. "They tend to drive out all true religion from the world, while man that is so bad is the maker of it; and it may be suspected to be bad, that is made by so bad an author.

8. "And it takes off the fear of God, and His judgment: for it is man that must be feared, so far as man is the maker of the law.

9. "And it destroys the consolation of believers, which consists in the hopes of a reward from God; for he that serves man, must be rewarded by man; and though they do not exclude God, but join him with themselves, yet this mixture debases and destroys religion, as the mixture of God and mammon in men's love, and as mixed and debased metals do the sovereign's coin.

10. "It hardens infidels and hinders their conversion; for they will reverence no more of our religion than we can prove to be divine: and when they find one part of it to be human, they suspect the rest to be so too, and condemn it all; even as protestants do popery, for the abundance of human trinkets and toys with which we see them exercise and delude their silly followers.

11. "It is the great engine of dividing all the church, and breeding and feeding contentions in the Christian world.

12. "And because men that will command, will be obeyed, and they that are absolutely subjected to God will obey none against Him, whatever it cost them, Dan. 3:6, Heb. 11, Lk. 14:26, 33, Mat. 5:10–12, therefore it has proved the occasion of bloody persecutions in the churches, by which professed Christians draw the guilt of Christian blood upon themselves.

13. "And hereby it has dolefully hindered the gospel, while the persecutors have silenced many worthy, conscionable preachers of it.

14. "And by this it has quenched charity in the hearts of both sides, and taught the sufferers and the afflicters to be equally bitter in censuring if not detesting one another.

15. "And the infidels seeing these dissensions and bitter passions among Christians deride and scorn, and hate them all.

16. "Yes, such causes as these in the Latin and Greek churches have engaged not only emperors and princes against their own subjects, so that chronicles and books of martyrs perpetuate their dishonor, as Pilate's name is in the creed; but also have set them in bloody wars among themselves.

17. "These have been the fruits, and this is the tendency of usurping Christ's prerogative over His religion and worship in His church."

CHAPTER EIGHT

MUSICAL INSTRUMENTS
AND THE WORSHIP OF GOD

Praise the Lord!
Praise God in His sanctuary;
Praise Him in His mighty expanse.
Praise Him for His mighty deeds;
Praise Him according to His excellent greatness.
Praise Him with trumpet sound;
Praise Him with harp and lyre.
Praise Him with timbrel and dancing;
Praise Him with stringed instruments and pipe.
Praise Him with loud cymbals;
Praise Him with resounding cymbals.
Let everything that has breath praise the Lord.
Praise the Lord! (Psalm 150)

Why do we use musical instruments in the worship of God? Should we use musical instruments in the worship of God? For most Christians today the answer to these questions is so obvious, that they need not even be asked. They help us worship God! But, how do we know that they help us worship God? Is this wishful thinking?

These questions are necessary ones because we may worship God only as He has commanded in His Word, with no additions or subtractions (Deut. 12:32). We may not do in worship anything He has not commanded. Furthermore, nothing helps us worship God but what He has commanded and instituted in the Bible. Everything man invents for whatever reason is a hindrance to worship and has the opposite effect—it encourages the worship of the human will, which is the source of any man-made additions to worship (Col. 2:16–23).

Why *do* we use musical instruments in the worship of God? Answer: God has commanded us to do so in the Bible, in such places as Psalm 150. In this psalm we are commanded to praise God for His excellent greatness in His sanctuary with every musical instrument suitable for worship.

Why did God command the use of musical instruments in worship? He did so for at least four reasons.

First, God commanded the use of musical instruments to assist us in the singing of His praises in worship. Many of the psalms are written to the choir director and list at the beginning of the psalm the musical instrument that is best suited to accompany that particular psalm. Psalm 4 is best accompanied with stringed instruments, Psalm 5 with flute accompaniment, Psalm 6 with stringed instruments, upon an eight-stringed lyre, and Psalm 12 is best accompanied with an eight-stringed lyre.

Second, God loves music. Music surrounds His throne in heaven (Rev. 5:8–9; 14:1–4). He invented it and put it in the hearts of human beings to create music and musical instruments, and to write and play beautiful music. He also created man and woman in His image so they would enjoy and be affected by music.

Third, the public worship of God is not only to be pure and unmixed with the traditions of men, it must also be beautiful and joyful in its music. Simplicity of worship according to the regulative principle of worship does not in any way imply that worship is to be drab, ugly, austere, and boring. biblical worship is to be filled with beautiful, joyful, and inspiring music. We see this particularly in the worship services of Israel during the reign of King David.

> All these were under the direction of their father to sing in the house of the Lord, with cymbals, harps and lyres, for the service of the house of God. Asaph, Jeduthun and Heman were under the direction of the king. Their number who were trained in singing to the Lord, with their relatives, all who were skillful, was 288. (1 Chronicles 25:6–7)

> When the priests came forth from the holy place (for all the priests who were present had sanctified themselves, without regard to divisions), and all the Levitical singers, Asaph, Heman, Jeduthun, and their sons and kinsmen, clothed in fine linen, with cymbals, harps and lyres, standing east of the altar, and with them one hundred and twenty priests blowing trumpets, in unison when the trumpeters and the singers were to make themselves heard with one voice to praise and to glorify the Lord, and when they lifted up their voice accompanied by trumpets and cymbals and instruments of music, and when they praised the Lord saying, "He indeed is good for His lovingkindness is everlasting," then the house, the house of the Lord, was filled with a cloud, so that the priests could not stand to minister because of the cloud, for the glory of the Lord filled the house of God. (2 Chronicles 5:11–14)

What beautiful and joyful music this must have been in the worship of God—choirs, hundreds of trained musicians, and singing accompanied with a variety of musical instruments! And God was so pleased with this service that He made His presence in the service known to the people worshipping Him, for the glory of the Lord filled the house of God.

No greater joy can be experienced than when God condescends in lovingkindness to meet with His people in their worship of Him, which is filled with beautiful music.

> So it was David, with the elders of Israel and the captains over thousands, who went to bring up the ark of the covenant of the Lord from the house of Obed-edom with joy. Because God was helping the Levites who were carrying

the ark of the covenant of the Lord, they sacrificed seven
bulls and seven rams. Now David was clothed with a robe of
fine linen with all the Levites who were carrying the ark, and
the singers and Chenaniah the leader of the singing with the
singers. David also wore an ephod of linen. Thus all Israel
brought up the ark of the covenant of the Lord with
shouting, and with sound of the horn, with trumpets, with
loud-sounding cymbals, with harps and lyres. It happened
when the ark of the covenant of the Lord came to the city of
David, that Michal the daughter of Saul looked out of the
window, and saw King David leaping and making merry, and
she despised him in her heart. And they brought in the ark of
God and placed it inside the tent which David had pitched
for it; and they offered burnt offerings and peace offerings
before God. (1 Chronicles 15:25–16:1)

When the Ark of the Covenant was brought to its
appointed location, Israel's praise of the Lord was exuberant,
because it was the symbol and pledge of the presence of the
Lord with His covenant people. By it He reassured the faithful
that He was their reconciled God who would enjoy friendly
communion with them in their worship of Him. How can
anyone who realizes that, in worship God fellowships with His
people, be anything but joyful in worship?

Fourth, 1 Chronicles 15:16 specifically states the purpose
of choirs and musical instruments in the worship of God:
"Then David spoke to the chiefs of the Levites to appoint their
relatives the singers, with instruments of music, harps, lyres,
loud-sounding cymbals, to raise sounds of joy," i.e., to heighten
the sound, both of the song and of the instrumental music, to
the expression of festive joy in the Lord and His works. John
Calvin, who believed that music was a gift of God, wrote that
music "has the power to enter the heart like wine poured into a
vessel, with good or evil effect." In worship in particular, "it has
great force and vigor to move and inflame the hearts of men to
invoke and praise God with a more vehement and ardent
zeal."[172] John Frame has pointed out that "Psalm 150 is
especially clear that the instruments are an accompaniment to
praise and are themselves means of praise."[173] We are to "praise
Him with trumpet sound...with harp and lyre... with timbrel

and dancing . . . with stringed instruments and pipe... with loud cymbals...with resounding cymbals" (Ps. 150:3–5).

In 1657, some of the participants in the Westminster Assembly in London, who gave us the *Westminster Confession of Faith and Catechisms* in the 1640s, published a lengthy, annotated commentary on the entire Bible. Their comment on Psalm 150 is worth quoting: "[God] exhorts them that they might praise God the better, to stir up their joy with musical instruments. And if musical instruments . . . had the power then; how have they changed their nature since?" This quote is an interesting one because it shows the attitude of these men toward the use of musical instruments in the worship of God— they were for it!

For the next couple of centuries, Presbyterians in Scotland and America refused to use musical instruments in worship believing it sinful. Several books and tracts were written to defend their position. This viewpoint largely prevailed throughout the nineteenth century. One major denomination continues to hold this view, the Reformed Presbyterian Church in North America, Covenanter.

Why do some reformed churches hold this view? They argue that because musical instruments were part of the temple worship of the Old Testament with all its symbolic rites and sacrifices of the Levitical ceremonial system, when that whole system reached its designed termination point in the life, death, and resurrection of Jesus Christ, the symbolic rites and sacrifices, along with temple with its musical instruments, were all abrogated and therefore, are no longer to be used in Christian worship. These were "shadows." Now the "substance," which is Christ, has come and there is no further need for observance of the shadows. Therefore, just as we no longer sacrifice animals in our worship services, nor go to the Temple in Jerusalem to worship, neither do we use the temple's musical instruments in Christian worship.

A closer look at this belief reveals several problems. One difficulty is that in the temple worship of the Old Testament, there were not only ceremonial elements, but also non-ceremonial elements that should always be included in the worship of God, such as prayer and praise. Just because one aspect of Old Testament worship has ceased to be applicable should we conclude that every aspect of Old Testament worship is inapplicable? Prayer and praise continue to be important elements of Christian worship. Although these were elements in temple worship, they did not cease when Christ brought the ceremonies of the temple to an end.

A second problem with this view of excluding musical instruments in worship is this: in what way were choirs and musical instruments in the temple ceremonial foreshadows and prophetic types of Christ and His accomplishment of redemption? Israel used musical instruments in celebrating the saving mercy of God in their behalf before God gave Moses the blueprints of the tabernacle and the ceremonial system. "Miriam the prophetess, Aaron's sister, took the timbrel in her hand, and all the women went out after her with timbrels and dancing" (Ex. 15:20). Although this did not take place in a worship service, the point is that Israel was accustomed to using musical instruments in their singing of God's praises long before tabernacle worship was established. In fact, the great choirs and multitude of musical instruments were instituted for the public worship of God five hundred years after Moses, during the reigns of David and Solomon. These were not a part of the Mosaic ceremonial system. The reason that system passed off the scene was because it was fulfilled in Christ. But the question remains, what is there about musical instruments that are typical or symbolic of Christ? That question has yet to be answered by those who hold the "non-instrumental" view of public worship.

Regarding the ceremonial and non-ceremonial elements of temple worship in the Old Testament, Ron Kirby gives this helpful insight:

It seems that a better way to look at the question would be to say that God, in the Temple worship, showed us how He is pleased to be worshipped, and that therefore all the elements

of Temple worship should inform our worship today. Even if
we consider the element of sacrifice, we must say that our
worship today must be centered upon the offering of a pure
sacrifice to God, for "without the shedding of blood there is
no forgiveness," Hebrews 9:22. Of course, the way we bring
such a sacrifice to God has changed; we no longer bring
animals as sacrifices, but we come to God pleading the blood
of the one Sacrifice for sins. The sacrifice has not been
abolished, but it has been transformed. It is the same with
other elements of OT worship, including instrumental
music. God has shown us that instrumental music in worship
pleases Him, and so we continue to use it, unless there are
biblical grounds for its cessation.[174]

In conclusion, God commands us in Psalm 150 to use every
suitable musical instrument available to us, along with gifted
musicians, in congregational worship. And they are to be
played well by those who are trained in them. King David made
sure that those who sang in the choirs and who played the
musical instruments were trained and skillful (1 Chron. 25:6–
7).

When God issues a command, we are to obey that
command until He says it is no longer in effect. God has
nowhere in Scripture annulled the command of Psalm 150. In
fact, the command is illustrated and enforced in the pictures of
the church's consummated worship in the presence of God:

> And when He had taken the book, the four living creatures
> and the twenty-four elders fell down before the Lamb, each
> one having a harp...And they sang a new song... "Worthy
> are you to take the book and to break its seals; for You were
> slain and purchased by God with Your blood men from every
> tribe and tongue and people and nation. (Revelation 5:8–9)

> Then I looked, and behold, the Lamb was standing on
> Mount Zion, and with Him one hundred and forty-four
> thousand, having His name and the name of His Father
> written on their foreheads. And I heard a voice from heaven,
> like the sound of many waters and like the sound of loud
> thunder, and the voice which I heard was like the sound of
> harpists playing on their harps. And they sang a new song
> before the throne...and no one could learn the song except

the one hundred and forty-four thousand who had been purchased from the earth. These are the ones...who follow the Lamb wherever He goes. (Revelation 14:1–4)

And I saw something like a sea of glass mixed with fire, and those who had been victorious over the beast and his image . . . standing on the sea of glass, holding harps of God. And they sang the song of Moses . . . and the song of the Lamb, saying,

> "Great and marvelous are Your works,
> O Lord God, the Almighty;
> Righteous and true are Your ways,
> King of the nations.
> Who will not fear, O Lord, and glorify Your name?
> For You alone are holy;
> For all the nations will come and worship before Your,
> For Your righteous acts have been revealed."

(Revelation 15:2–4)

CHAPTER NINE

DID PAUL DO AWAY WITH
THE FOURTH COMMANDMENT?

The Epistle to the Colossians was written by the apostle Paul to combat false teachers who were trying to confuse the church in Colossae with a syncretistic worldview, a blending of Christianity with other religions and philosophies: a little bit of Christianity, (but with a low view of Christ), a little bit of the Old Testament, (wrongly interpreted), some legalistic Jewish ceremonialism, some Platonic angelolatry, and a lot of asceticism. In this chapter, we will focus on the Jewish ceremonialism and how Paul deals with it.

Jewish ceremonialism refers to those rituals, such as circumcision, and those holy days of the Jewish calendar, that were connected with religious feasts and convocations, all of which were commanded by Jehovah to be observed by Israel in the Old Testament. They were designed with a specific purpose and a specific termination point. Their purpose was to be foreshadows and prophetic symbols of Jesus Christ and His accomplishment of redemption in the New Covenant. Therefore, they were destined to come to an end with the life, death, and resurrection of Christ. As Paul says in Colossians 2:17, they were the shadows but Christ is the substance, or body, that cast those shadows; so that when He came on the scene of history, they passed off the scene.

The problem for the apostolic church in the days of Paul was that there were converts to Christianity from Judaism who were so accustomed to the Old Testament calendar of holy days and religious feasts that they continued to practice many of these things after they had become members of the Christian Church. For example, they observed the Sabbath on Saturday according to Jewish practice, and they celebrated the resurrection on the Lord's Day, every first day of the week according to the Christian practice. They practiced circumcision and baptism.

The time period to which we are referring lasted only a few years. It consisted of the years of transition from the Old Testament era to the New Testament era. Many Christians during that interim lived in both times. They were Jewish before Christ's death and resurrection, and they were Christian afterward. So God had Paul counsel the church on how to handle the various transitional situations.

In circumstances where the Jewish Christians had not come into a full understanding of Christ and the New Covenant and its relation to the Old Testament era, or where new Christians were hesitant to give up the Old Testament calendar and circumcision, Paul would allow them to continue to do so as he and other teachers gave them further instruction leading them into Christian maturity. In Romans 14:1–6, he instructs the "weak," who still practiced some of the old ceremonies, not to judge the "strong," and more mature Christian with a more complete understanding, as "less spiritual" because they did not practice the old ceremonies. And he instructs the "strong" not to be insensitive toward the "weak."

However, in the Galatian churches, things were different. There, false teachers were trying to impose Jewish rituals and the Jewish calendar on the churches as requirements for salvation, along with faith in Christ. We call them Judaizers. In Galatians 4:9–12, Paul warns the Galatian Christians about being seduced by this Jewish legalism, which amounted to the Judaizing of Christianity.

In the church at Colossae, the situation was different still. False teachers were trying to seduce this church into blending several religious and philosophical elements with Christianity that would eventually destroy Christianity there. One of those elements was Jewish ceremonialism. Paul exhorts them: "Therefore no one is to act as your judge in regard to food or drink or in respect to a festival or a new moon or a Sabbath day—things which are a mere shadow of what is to come; but the substance belongs to Christ" (Col. 2:16–17). (Sabbath day is an inaccurate translation of the Greek. The word for Sabbath is plural, hence it would be more accurately translated Sabbaths.)

In these verses, "Paul repudiates any required observance of Jewish religious days or festivals, asserting that the church may not require the observance of any Old Testament ceremonial day, because they were 'a mere shadow' of what is to come; but the substance belongs to Christ."[175] These Old Testament ceremonies foreshadowed Christ. And now that we have Christ, we do not need to observe the shadows. As our *Westminster Confession of Faith* states: "Under the new testament, the liberty of Christians is further enlarged, in their freedom from the yoke of the ceremonial law, to which the Jewish Church was subjected" (XX, I). And why does our *Westminster Confession* say this? Behind all the Old Testament observances stands the person and work of Christ. Each of these ceremonial days, festivals, and rituals pointed to Him. Therefore when He came, He was the fulfillment of them all and in fulfilling them, placed the Jewish ceremonies "out of gear." He thus placed the church in a better, freer, and fuller relation to God than Old Testament believers had.

Why bring all this up? Because our text, Colossians 2:16, says, "No one is to act as your judge in regard to food or drink or in respect to a festival or a new moon or Sabbath day." In the first part of the verse, Paul is referring to the practices of asceticism and in the second part to the practices of Jewish ceremonialism. His warning is this: Because all we need we have in Christ (2:3; 9–10), we must not submit ourselves to man-made rules and regulations; and we must not return to Jewish ceremonialism, for Christ has set us free from both.

The point is obvious enough, but, amazingly, Colossians 2:16 is misused and perverted by most of the Christian church today. It is used to support the belief that now that Christ has come and placed believers under grace, we are no longer under any of the Old Testament laws. Most especially, we are no longer obligated to keep the Sabbath commands, not even on Sunday. Now, they tell us, all days are alike, holy unto the Lord, and the Fourth Commandment no longer applies to us. Therefore, these folks would have us disregard the Old Testament laws regarding Sabbath observance, and believe that what the *Westminster Confession* and *Catechisms* say on the subject are legalistic and should be disregarded as well. On Sunday, or whatever day is suitable to our situation, the anti-regulativists say we should celebrate the resurrection of Christ with our families and with other believers, but beyond that, Sunday is just another day to do as we please. They say that Sabbath keeping robs Christians of their liberty in Christ. As one man told me after a sermon I preached on keeping the Christian Sabbath: "I have been set free from the Law of God and I will not come back under its bondage in Sabbath observance!"

What is at stake here is fundamental to Christianity. Voltaire, the French atheist, understood the importance of the Christian Sabbath better than most American Christians, when he said that if the revolutionaries were going to succeed in destroying Christianity in France, they must first destroy the Christian Sabbath, which he recommended.

The three terms in Colossians 2:16, festival, new moon, or Sabbath day, are often used together in the Old Testament for the various ceremonial days and feasts Jehovah commanded Israel to observe. He also appointed the king's portion of his goods for the burnt offerings, namely, for the morning and evening burnt offerings, and the burnt offerings for the Sabbaths and for the new moons and for the fixed festivals, as it is written in the Law of the Lord (2 Chron. 31:3).

Leviticus 23 is a commentary on the entire liturgical calendar of the Old Testament church. Leviticus 23:1–3 indicates that "Sabbaths" include the seventh day Sabbath. Leviticus 23:4–44 explains the great festivals of the Old Testament church: Passover, the Feast of Unleavened Bread, the Feast of Pentecost, and the Feast of Booths. And Leviticus 23:24–25 speak of special observances to be performed on the first day of the month. It is these services that Paul has in mind when he uses the phrase, "new moons." "Thus by these three phrases, Paul is describing the Old Testament ceremonial days and Sabbaths and says that the Christian is under no obligation to observe these days."[176]

To be specific, Paul is abrogating the observance of the seventh-day Sabbath, along with the other holy days of the Old Testament ceremonial calendar, but not the moral principle involved in the Fourth Commandment. The Christian is no longer obligated to observe the seventh day Sabbath. "The New Testament repeals the seventh-day observance, but never the obligation of keeping one day in seven as the Sabbath."[177] How do we know this? Paul is concerned here with the Christian's relation to the ceremonial laws of the Old Testament, not with the moral laws of God. The Christian's celebration of the Lord's Day on the first day of the week is not even in question in Colossians, Rome, or Galatia. The observance of Sunday as the Lord's Day was universally understood and practiced by the apostolic church. There was no disagreement about its sanctity by Gentile Christians or Jewish Christians. Paul's concern in Colossians is with Saturday, not Sunday.

When Paul condemns the requiring of Christians to keep holy days, Sabbaths, new moons, and festivals of the Old Testament, he is referring to those days under debate and no others. His concern is with the distinctive elements of the Old Testament dispensation of the Covenant that pointed to Christ and were fulfilled by Him, not with the honoring of Sunday as the Lord's Day.

So then, the New Testament changes the day but preserves the Sabbath for Christians in accordance with the claims of Christ who said: "The Sabbath was made for man, and not man for the Sabbath. So the Son of Man is Lord even of the Sabbath" (Mark 2:27–28). His point is that the Sabbath command remains in force in Christ's kingdom, for it is of benefit to mankind. As long as Christ has a kingdom, He will have a Sabbath, over which He is Lord, because the Sabbath was made, not exclusively for Israel, but for man, i.e., the entire human race. In the Isaiah 66:22–23 prophecy concerning the present reign of Christ we find the following declaration: "'For just as the new heavens and the new earth which I will make will endure before Me,' declares the LORD, 'So your offspring and your name will endure. And it shall be from new moon to new moon and from sabbath to sabbath, all mankind will come to bow down before Me,' says the LORD." Critics of the continuing Sabbath principle become irrational in their explanation of Jesus' words. They say that Christ's claiming lordship over the Sabbath was for the purpose of getting rid of it whenever He wanted, and thus He abolished it.

Hebrews 4:9–10 also speaks to the continuity of the morality of observing the Sunday-Sabbath as the Lord's Day, as over against a continuing seventh day Sabbath. *So there remains therefore a Sabbath rest for the people of God. For the One who has entered His rest has Himself also rested from His works, as God did from His.*

Hebrews 4 speaks of the rest from the tyranny and guilt of sin we have through faith in Jesus Christ. The words, "rest" or "rested" occur ten times in this chapter, and every time but one the Greek noun, *katapausis*, or its verb, is used. The one exception is in verse 9, where the Greek word for Sabbath rest is *sabbatismos*. When this noun or its verb form is used in the Septuagint, it also carries the idea of "Sabbath keeping" or "Sabbath observance," as in Leviticus 23:32. It is to be a Sabbath of complete rest to you, and you shall humble your souls . . . from evening until evening you shall keep your sabbath." Therefore in addition to the *katapausis* (rest) all believers have in Christ, we also have a *sabbatismos* (Sabbath keeping) to celebrate our spiritual and eternal *katapausis*. "Because the promised rest lies ahead for the New Covenant people of God, they are to strive to enter the future rest, 4:11. Yet as they do, they anticipate it by continuing to keep the Sabbath."[178]

Verse 10 gives us the basis and explanation for verse 9. It begins with for, or because. Believers have a continuing Sabbath to keep because of what is spoken of in verse 10. Verse 9 establishes the continuing Sabbath principle and verse 10 establishes the day this Sabbath rest is to be observed. Verse 10 contrasts the rest of Christ from His redemptive labors on the first day of the week, when He arose from the dead, with the rest of God from His creative labors on the seventh day of the creation week, when He took delight in His handiwork. "And God rested on the seventh day from all His works" (Heb. 4:4). So then, verse 10 should be translated: "For the One (Christ) who has entered His (Christ's) rest (from His redemptive work) has Himself also rested from His (redemptive) works, as God did from His (creative works)." In other words, verse 10 links the believer's continuing Sabbath obligation with the Lord's Day, the first day of the week when Jesus arose from the dead. On the first day of the week, the day of His resurrection, Jesus rested from His redemptive work, as God rested from His creating work on the seventh day of the week, the Old Testament Sabbath. So then, we may reasonably conclude that the day of the week for the Sabbath has changed from the seventh to the first day, in order to commemorate the resurrection of Christ, and that the Sabbath itself continues for the believer in Christ. The Sabbath, as the Fourth Commandment requires, still comes one day in seven, but now it is on Sunday.

What exactly are the reasons for this interpretation of Hebrews 4:10?

First, in Hebrews 3:7–4:11, the author speaks of those believers who enjoy rest in Christ in the plural. "Therefore, let us fear if, while a promise remains of entering His rest . . . For we who have believed enter that rest . . . Therefore let us be diligent to enter that rest" (Heb. 4:1, 3, 11). But in verse 10 he refers to a singular individual, i.e., someone other than the people of God referred to in verse 9. Second, verse 10 speaks of a completed rest enjoyed by this one, while verse 11 says that believers, who possess spiritual rest from sin now by faith, nevertheless must wait for the completion of their rest when they enter heaven. The singular individual enjoys complete rest now; believers must wait for complete rest in the future.

Third, the common interpretation of verse 10 is mistaken. It holds that the identity of the one who has entered His rest has himself also rested from his works is the believer who has entered rest from sin through faith in Christ, and who has therefore rested or repented from his sinful and unrighteous works that once dominated his life before he became a believer. Now, why is this interpretation impossible? It is improper to compare the evil works of a sinner with the good works of God. It approaches blasphemy "to compare a sinner's works of sin and self-righteousness to the work of a holy God in creation."[179] Where in the entire New Testament is it even remotely suggested that repentance (rest and cessation) from evil works is analogous to God's resting from His creative works? The two "rests" are not even comparable. The believer who repents of his sin ceases from his evil works, makes a clean break with them, and hates the life of evil works that he once lived. In complete contrast, when God rested from His creating, organizing, and beautifying the world with light, order, and life, He took great delight in His work, loving the display of His glory in it.

Therefore, since the entire Bible is the Word of God, we must not interpret one passage in a way that contradicts another. And, further, we must always interpret the difficult passages in the light of the clear passages where the meaning is more obvious. Therefore, we cannot interpret Colossians 2:16 as saying anything that contradicts Jesus' statements in Hebrews 4:9, 10, or any other Scripture for that matter. Rather, Paul in Colossians 2:6 is condemning the required observation of the Old Testament ceremonial calendar with its holy days and Sabbath, including the seventh day Sabbath, *not* the abiding morality of the Fourth Commandment. The day is changed, but the Sabbath is preserved!

So now, to sum up, what do we know about the Sabbath command and the celebration of the Lord's Day?

1. The Sabbath was a creation ordinance predating the ceremonial laws of Moses (Gen. 2:2). Sabbath observance did not begin at Mount. Sinai, hence we are told in the Fourth Command to remember the Sabbath...

2. The Sabbath commandment is incorporated in the heart of the Ten Commandments, as the longest of the ten. In fact it is so embedded in the Ten Commandments that to regard it as of a different character from the other nine with reference to its abiding relevance, contradicts the unity and significance of what was written on the two tablets of stone. It is highly arbitrary to label the Fourth Commandment as ceremonial and therefore temporary, while considering the other nine as moral and therefore permanent.

3. The antinomian would have us believe that "the pattern provided by God (Gen. 2:2, 3) in the work of creation (cf. also Exodus 20:11; 31:17) has no longer any relevance for the regulation of man's life on earth, that only nine of the ten words of the Decalogue have authority for Christians, that the beneficent design contemplated in the original institution (Mark 2:28) has no application under the gospel, and that the lordship of Christ exercised over the Sabbath was for the purpose of abolishing it as an institution to be observed... There is no evidence to support any of these conclusions, and, when they are combined and their cumulative force frankly weighed, it is then that the whole analogy of Scripture is shown to be contradicted by the assumption concerned."[180]

4. The first day of the week, as the day Jesus arose from the grave, has a special significance in the New Testament *because* it is the day Jesus arose from the grave.

The decisive instance illustrating this point is the Day of Pentecost recorded in Acts 1 and 2. Pentecost was an Old Testament religious festival. Its date was fixed in the following manner: on the first day of the week after the Sabbath of the Passover week (Lev. 23:15–16, Deut.16:9), "a sheaf of the earliest ripe corn was cut, brought fresh into the sanctuary, and presented as a thank-offering to God. Thus the day of this ceremonial must always be the first day of the week, corresponding to the Lord's Day. From this day they were to count seven weeks complete, and the fiftieth day was to be Pentecost day, or the beginning of their 'feast of ingathering.'"[181] This means that the day of Pentecost was the first day of the week after seven weeks of seven days.

Christ arose on the first day of the week. According to Acts 1 and 2, the day selected by God for the baptism of the church with the Holy Spirit was the Day of Pentecost, which took place on a Sunday, in fact the seventh Sunday since Christ's resurrection. Therefore, according to Acts 1:12 and 2:1, "this seventh Lord's day, (Sunday), was also employed by apostles and disciples as a day for religious worship; and it was while they were thus engaged that they received the divine sanction in their blessed baptism of fire and of the Holy Ghost. Then the first public proclamation of the gospel under the new dispensation began, and the model was set up for the consecration of the new Christian Sabbath—not by the burning of additional lambs—by public preaching, the two sacraments of baptism and the supper, and the oblation of their worldly substance to God. At this all-important stage every step, every act, of the divine providence recorded by inspiration in the Acts was formative and fundamental. Hence we must believe that this event was meant by God as a forcible precedent, establishing the Lord's Day as our Christian Sabbath."[182]

Now on the first day of the week Mary Magdalene came early to the tomb, while it was still dark, and saw the stone already taken away from the tomb...When it was evening on that day, the first day of the week, and when the doors were shut where the disciples were, for fear of the Jews, Jesus came and stood in their midst, and said to them, "Peace be with you." ...And after eight days His disciples were again inside, and Thomas with them. Jesus came, the doors having been shut, and stood in their midst, and said, "Peace be with you." (John 20:1, 19, 26)

Immediately after Christ's resurrection on the first day of the week, the disciples already attribute a particular importance to Sunday. On the evening of the very Sunday Jesus arose from the grave, they were meeting together. This is the beginning of the Lord's Day. Then, eight days later, or on the first day of the second week after Jesus' resurrection, the disciples have gathered again. The resurrected Christ confirmed their practice by personally appearing in their gatherings during the forty days between His resurrection and His ascension (John 20:19, 26).

John's Gospel speaks of the disciples meeting on the day of Christ's resurrection—the first day of the week—and then of their meeting eight days later. The "first day" and the "eighth day" are linked in the symbolism of the Old Testament ceremonial calendar. We see this in Leviticus 23:34-39, "On the fifteenth of this seventh month is the Feast of Booths for seven days to the LORD. On the first day is a holy convocation; you shall do no laborious work of any kind. For seven days you shall present an offering by fire to The LORD. On the eighth day you shall have a holy convocation and present an offering by fire to the LORD; it is an assembly. You shall do no laborious work...On exactly the fifteenth day of the seventh month, when you have gathered in the crops of the land, you shall celebrate the feast of the LORD for seven days, with a Sabbath rest on the first day and a Sabbath rest on the eighth day."

The Feast of Booths was a feast of joy and thanksgiving to the Lord. The Feast of Pentecost (23:15), symbolized the gathering of the first fruits of the world harvest of the elect from all nations; and the Feast of Booths symbolized the completion of the universal and final harvest and the newness of consummated life in the kingdom of Christ. It is for this reason that the first day of the week played such a symbolic role in the rituals of this Feast. Our text speaks of the fifteenth day, which is the first day of the week after two weeks of seven days; the first day, and closely connected with this the eighth day, which is the first day of the week after one week of seven days. Each of these "first day Sabbaths" in the Old Testament ceremonial calendar symbolized the newness and consummation of life in the kingdom of Christ. They are also days of holy convocation and the assembly of the congregation of the Lord in public worship (23:36).

The symbolism of "the first day" and "the eighth day" shaped Christian thinking about the Lord's Day. It was for this reason that John spoke of the resurrected Jesus Christ meeting with His gathered disciples on the first day and then again eight days later. These first days of the week still were considered days of holy convocation for the Christian church to celebrate the resurrection of Christ, who would come to them and minister to them in their worship services. These "first day Sabbaths" fit perfectly in the new day, new life, new dispensation, new creation, and new heavens and earth, which Jesus Christ put into place. With the life, death, resurrection, and ascension of Jesus Christ, the consummation has begun (Heb. 9:26), and the ingathering of the elect of God from the four corners of the earth (Matt. 24:31), and it shall advance First Day of the week by First Day of the week until the Second Coming of Christ at the very end of the world which begins God's "Eighth Day" of eternal Sabbath for His people in the bliss of His presence (Isa. 66:23).

As the apostles understood the symbolism of the first day and the eighth day by inspiration, they changed the day for celebrating the eternal rest and newness of life in the resurrected Christ from the seventh day to the first day, with Christ's full authority since they were infallibly inspired by Christ's own Holy Spirit.

The point is that apostolic "example may be as valid and instructive a guide to duty as precept. Or, to state it in another form, the precedent set by Christ and His apostles may be as binding as their command. The other is that whatever necessarily follows from Scripture *by good and necessary consequence* is as really authorized by it as *what is expressly set down*. (WCF 1.6)"[183]

> And on the first day of the week, when we were gathered
> together to break bread, Paul began talking to them,
> intending to depart the next day, and he prolonged his
> message until midnight. (Acts 20:7)

It was the custom for the apostolic church to meet for worship on the first day of the week. According to Acts 20:7, they gathered together to hear apostolic doctrine and to celebrate the Lord's Supper (Acts 2:42). The following points should be noted about this verse: (1) The assembly of disciples took place on the first day of the week. (2) On Sunday the disciples were gathered together. The Greek word is the verbal root of the noun "synagogue," which is one of the New Testament words for the church as a worshipping community, gathered for holy Christian convocation (James 2:2). (3) To break bread is an allusion to the communion the early church shared with each other in Christ, manifested in the Lord's Supper and in "church suppers" (Acts 2:42, 46; 1 Cor. 11:20–22). (4) Paul's talking to them and the prolonging of his message refers to the apostolic preaching and teaching of the gospel of Christ. His message is *logon* in Greek, meaning the "word," such as in the phrase, the word of His grace (Acts 14:3), to which the apostles bore witness in their preaching.

It should also be observed that in returning from his missionary journey to Macedonia and Achaia, Paul stopped at Troas to spend a whole week with the church there. Paul preached at their worship service on the first day of the week, after waiting a whole week in Troas, which included a Saturday Sabbath. "Why did he wait a whole week? Why did not the meeting, with the sermon and sacrament, take place on the Jewish Sabbath? We learn from verse 16 that Paul had very little time to spare because he had to make the whole journey from Philippi to Jerusalem, with all his wayside visits, within the six weeks between the end of the paschal and the beginning of the Pentecostal feast. He was obviously waiting for the church's sacred day [the Lord's Day] in order to join them in their public worship."[184]

> Now concerning the collection for the saints, as I directed the churches of Galatia, so do you also. On the first day of every week let each one of you put aside and save, as he may prosper, that no collections be made when I come.
> (1 Corinthians 16:1–2)

Just as it was the practice in the Galatian churches, so also in the Corinthian church it was the practice to gather for worship the first day of every week. Along with the preaching of the Word and the administration of the sacraments, a collection was to be received every Lord's Day for the needy, every one was to participate, and the offerings were to be in proportion to the means of the giver. These principles were officially established for the churches by apostolic authority, which was representative of the authority of Christ.

I was in the Spirit on the Lord's Day. (Revelation 1:10)

The term the apostle John used, the Lord's Day, *kuriake hemera*, denotes a day that belongs uniquely to the Lord Jesus Christ. We are often told that this text does not explicitly identify the Lord's Day as Sunday. But it could not have been any other day of the week. The apostolic church recognized only the first day of the week, the day of the Lord's resurrection, as a day of singular religious significance, belonging uniquely to the Lord Jesus Christ. It is not the often-used phrase, "the day of the Lord," but a phrase that denotes a day belonging to the Lord. This same word is used in 1 Corinthians 11:20 for the Lord's Supper—a meal that belongs uniquely to the Lord Jesus Christ to celebrate His redeeming work and to communicate His redeeming grace to His people. "In like manner, the first day of the week is called the Lord's Day because it is a day that belongs peculiarly to the Lord and was appointed to commemorate His completed redemption and to communicate grace to His people."[185] The Lord's congregation meets on the Lord's Day to hear the Lord's Word and celebrate the Lord's Supper.

> The pagan magistrates had banished [John] to this rocky, desolate, islet [Patmos] in the Aegean Sea as a punishment for preaching the gospel and testifying that Jesus is our risen Savior. He was there alone, separated from all his brethren. But he was in the Spirit on the Lord's Day. What does that mean? It means that he was doing what godly people now call "keeping Sunday." He was engaging in spiritual exercises. He was holding communion with the Holy Spirit. Here, then, is our first point: that although in solitude, cut off alike from Christian meetings and ordinary week-day occupations, by his banishment, the inspired apostle was "keeping Sunday." It is the strongest possible example. Our second point is that God blessed him in his Sabbath-keeping with the greatest spiritual blessing which perhaps he had enjoyed since he sat at the feet of Jesus. His Savior came down from glory to "keep Sunday" with him. Our third and strongest point is that the inspired man here calls the day the Lord's Day. There is no doubt but that the "Lord" named is the glorified Redeemer . . . There is but one consistent and Scriptural sense to place on this name of the day. It is the day that belongs especially to the Lord. But as all our days belong in one sense to Him, the only meaning is that the first day of the week is now set apart and hallowed to Christ. (Robert L. Dabney)[186]

The Lord's Day, on the first day of week is the one and only day of every week to which is given distinctive religious significance by the apostolic church. "Since it occurs every seventh day, it is a perpetually recurring memorial with religious intent and character proportionate to the place which Jesus' resurrection occupies in the accomplishment of redemption. The two pivotal events in this accomplishment are the death and resurrection of Christ and the two memorial ordinances of the New Testament institution are the Lord's Supper and the Lord's Day, the one memorializing Jesus' death and the other His resurrection. If Paul in Romans 14:5 [and Colossians 2:16] implies that all distinctions of days have been obliterated, then there is no room for the distinctive significance of the first day of the week as the Lord's Day. The evidence supporting the memorial character of the first day is not to be control and consequently, in this respect also the assumption in question cannot be entertained, namely, that all religious distinction of days is completely abrogated in the Christian economy."[187]

Therefore, when Paul rebukes the required observance of the Old Testament Sabbaths, new moons and festivals, he cannot be including the Lord's Day as the Christian's new Sabbath. To place the Lord's Day and the holy days of the Hebrew calendar in the same category "is not only to go beyond the warrant of exegetical requirements, but it brings us into conflict with principles that are embedded in the total witness of Scripture. An interpretation that involves such contradiction cannot be adopted."[188] Therefore, Colossians 2:16 cannot be used by the antinomians to support their case.

CONCLUDING APPLICATION

First, the *Church of Christ* may not observe Saturday as the Sabbath, nor may it add any other holy days, or religious rites and festivals to the worship of God. Our *Westminster Directory of Public Worship* states in its appendix: "There is no day commanded in Scripture to be kept holy under the gospel but the Lord's Day, which is the Christian Sabbath. Festival days, called 'holy-days,' having no warrant in the Word of God, are not to be continued." Christ transformed everything. In Him we have all we need. We are complete in Him, and so we celebrate Him every Sunday, and no day in our calendar is as holy as this one. Every day is to be dedicated to the service of the Lord, but the Lord's Day belongs uniquely to Him.

In faithfulness to the biblical principles we have been discussing, the General Assembly of the Presbyterian Church in the United States in 1899 declared: "There is no warrant in Scripture for the observance of Christmas and Easter as holy days, rather the contrary, Galatians 4:9-11 and Colossians 2:16-21, and such observance is contrary to the principles of the reformed faith, conducive to will-worship, and not in harmony with the simplicity of the gospel of Jesus Christ."

Morton Smith, in his book, *How is the Gold Become Dim*, argues that the Presbyterian Church in the United States attitude of indifference toward the teaching of the Westminster Standards in areas such as this, led to her slide into apostasy. Now the same denomination not only repudiates its earlier decisions, but it has reversed itself to the point that it has adopted the liturgical calendar of past tradition without any biblical basis. In other words, once the regulative principle of worship is cast aside by a church, that church is on a slippery slope to apostasy.[189]

Second, Jesus Christ, through His Spirit-inspired apostles, changed the day but preserved the Sabbath principle of the Fourth Commandment for Christians in the Lord's Day on the first day of the every week. This is not only taught in such places as Hebrews 4, as we have seen, but it is also an inescapable inference that is necessarily deduced from four teachings in the Bible:

1. The Sabbath is a perpetual institution, being instituted by God for the human race at creation and republished in the Ten Commandments, which all people in all places are to obey. Jesus said that the Sabbath was made for man, and until heaven and earth pass away, not the smallest stroke or letter of His moral law will cease to have authority in our lives (Matt. 5:17f).

2. No man or church has the authority from God to institute a holy day of religious significance, e.g., Lent, Good Friday, Ash Wednesday, Christmas, Easter, etc. This is the point of Colossians 2:16.

3. The seventh day or Saturday Sabbath of the Old Testament is no longer the Sabbath, being left in the grave when Christ arose on the first day of the week, or Sunday. That is the point of Hebrews 4:9–10 and Colossians 2:16. Therefore The Church of Christ is

forbidden to have Saturday or any other day, but Sunday, as the Christian's Sabbath.

4. Christ and His apostles attributed to Sunday a special religious significance and importance as the Lord's Day, immediately after Christ's resurrection, to celebrate His resurrection. And Divine example is as authoritative as express Divine command.

Therefore, the only inference we can draw from these biblical truths, which the church has believed for two thousand years, is that the Lord's Day on the first day of every week is the Christian's Sabbath, established as such by the Son of God.

As our *Westminster Confession of Faith* so faithfully states: [God] has particularly appointed one day in seven, for a Sabbath to be kept holy unto Him: which, from the beginning of the world to the resurrection of Christ, was the last day of the week; and, from the resurrection of Christ, was changed to the first day of the week, which, in Scripture, is called the Lord's Day, and is to be continued to the end of the world, as the Christian Sabbath (XXI, VII).

CHAPTER TEN

WHAT SONGS SHOULD
BE SUNG DURING WORSHIP?

Let the peace of Christ rule in your hearts, to which indeed
you were called in one body; and be thankful. Let the word
of Christ richly dwell within you; with all wisdom, teaching
and admonishing one another with psalms and hymns and
spiritual songs, singing with thankfulness in your hearts to
God. Whatever you do in word or deed, do all in the name
of the Lord Jesus, giving thanks through Him to God the
Father. (Colossians 3:15–17, cf. Ephesians 5:19)

THE PROBLEMS WITH EXCLUSIVE PSALMODY

Some reformed Bible scholars argue that psalms and
hymns and spiritual songs refer solely to the 150 psalms in the
Old Testament; and therefore, only the 150 Psalms may be
sung in worship.[190] Their argument is twofold: These three
words occur frequently in the Greek Old Testament
(Septuagint) in the titles of the psalms; and the word, spiritual,
indicates that these three types of songs are Spirit-produced,
i.e., inerrantly inspired by the Holy Spirit. However, this
viewpoint, called exclusive psalmody, has many problems.[191]
First, this view presses the meaning of spiritual farther than it
can legitimately be pressed in this context. Second, it

unnecessarily restricts the meaning of psalms and hymns and spiritual songs. While it is true that the three terms are used in the psalm titles, it is also true that they are used outside the book of psalms. And many times these words do not refer to compositions in the book of Psalms.

Leonard Coppes has exposed the fundamental weaknesses of the theological exegesis for exclusive psalmody.[192] His points are as follows:

1. The theological method and conclusions expressed in exclusive psalmody reverse the order of the importance of preaching and singing. It does this by its conclusion that God regulates singing more closely than He regulates preaching. Biblically speaking, however, God teaches us that preaching occupies a more central and more important place in Christian worship.

2. The theological method and conclusions expressed in exclusive psalmody ignore the progress of biblical revelation.

3. The theological method and conclusions expressed in exclusive psalmody teach: God is pleased . . . when the Son is not honored in worship on par with the Father.[193]

4. The theological method and conclusions expressed in exclusive psalmody posit a difference between worship fulfilled in Christ and worship as practiced in heaven.

5. Those who maintain exclusive psalmody sometimes shift their argument to maintaining that the regulative principle limits us to singing inspired words exclusively but they maintain this on the basis of Ephesians 5:18–21 and Colossians 3:16–17. These verses say nothing about limiting our singing in church worship and, therefore, do not limit us to singing only inspired words...The same argument that allows us to speak and preach without simply quoting the Bible allows us to use words other than inspired words in singing in worship.

6. The theological method and conclusions expressed in exclusive psalmody mandate that certain Christians violate God's regulative principle. Linguists are quite familiar with languages that are tonal or musical. Those who speak such languages must either limit all their vocalizing in worship to the phrases of 150 psalms or they must violate God's regulative principle for worship.

THE MEANING OF PSALMS

The Hebrew Old Testament has four different nouns translated "psalm": *zimrah*, *zamir*, *mizmor*, and *tehillah*. Only *mizmor* occurs in the Hebrew titles of the Psalms, e.g., Psalm 3, 4, 5; while the others have both a general and specific sense.[194] *Mizmor*, therefore, is the technical word for psalms from the book of Psalms. Neither *zimrah* nor *zamir* occur in Psalm titles. It is important to note that nowhere in the Bible are we commanded to sing *mizmor*. Rather when the Bible commands us to sing to the Lord, it uniformly uses terms meaning "praise" in a general sense.

> Sing unto Him, sing psalms unto Him, talk ye of all His wondrous works. (Psalm 105:2 KJV)

Although the King James Version seems to say that we are commanded to sing psalms, no Hebrew word for psalm appears in this verse, (or in 1 Chronicles 16:9). The New American Standard Version translates it correctly as "sing praises to Him." The Hebrew verb here means "sing, sing praise, make music." This same verb occurs in Judges 5:3; Psalm 9:11, 18:49, 27:6, 30:4, 30:12, 47:7, 59:17, 75:9, 101:1, 104:33, 135:3, 146:2; and Isaiah 12:5. These are of a general nature commanding Christians to sing God's praise, not to sing exclusively Psalms.

> Sing unto the Lord with the harp; with the voice of a psalm. (Psalm 98:5 KJV)

> Take a psalm, and bring hither the timbrel, the pleasant harp with the psaltery. (Psalm 81:2 KJV)

The Hebrew word for "psalm" in these verses is *zimrah*, denoting melody or song in general. It also occurs in Exodus 15:2, Psalm 118:14, Isaiah 12:2, Isaiah 51:3, and Amos 5:23.

> Let us come before His presence with thanksgiving, and
> make a joyful noise unto Him with psalms. (Psalm 95:2 KJV)

In this verse, we have a Hebrew word identifying the content of our singing of praise, not the technical word, *mizmor*, but the more general word for songs, *zemirot*. This word does not always refer to the Old Testament Psalter when it is used in the Old Testament, e.g., Job 35:10, Psalm 119:54, Isaiah 24:16, Isaiah 25:5.

"In all these commands it is noteworthy that general terms meaning 'praise' are used. The authoritative Brown, Driver, and Briggs Lexicon does not even list "psalm" as a possible definition of *zimrah* or *zamir*. Exclusive Psalmodists have not proven the usage of the more restrictive sense: the Psalter."[195]

The Greek word for "psalm" is *psalmos*, having either the broad meaning of "song of praise," or the narrow meaning "psalm." It is related to the verb, *psallo*, meaning "sing (to the accompaniment of a harp), sing praise." It can refer to the whole book of Psalms, as in Luke 20:42 and Acts 1:20, or to a specific Psalm as in Acts 13:33, or to the whole section of the Old Testament, known as "the Writings," of which the book of Psalms is the largest book and which includes other books of the Old Testament (Luke 24:4). None of these passages we have just mentioned commands singing in worship.

> When you assemble, each one has a psalm, has a teaching,
> has a revelation, has a tongue, has an interpretation. Let all
> things be done for edification. (1 Corinthians 14:26)

Here psalm could be taken either in the general sense of a song of praise or in the narrow sense of a psalm. The context does not specify. What Paul is commanding is not the bringing of a psalm, doctrine, tongue, (and the like), but that everything in worship be done for edification.

> Is anyone among you suffering? Let him pray. Is anyone
> cheerful? He is to sing praises. (James 5:13)

The KJV has it: "let him sing psalms." However this verse
does not contain the noun "psalms." Rather, the verb *psallo* is
used, denoting, as we have seen, "sing (to the accompaniment
of a harp), sing praise." This verb can be translated simply: Let
him sing.

> Be filled with the Spirit; speaking to yourselves in psalms and
> hymns and spiritual songs, singing and making melody in
> your heart to the Lord. (Ephesians 5:18b–19 KJV)

> Let the word of Christ dwell in you richly in all wisdom;
> teaching and admonishing one another in psalms and hymns
> and spiritual songs, singing with grace in your hearts to the
> Lord. (Colossians 3:16 KJV)

Although the word "psalms" in these verses is used in a list
of various kinds of songs and probably refers to the Old
Testament Psalter, nevertheless neither text specifically refers
to public worship, nor confines the singing of these kinds of
songs to public worship. "But even granting that there is an
application in these verses to Christian worship, it must be
stressed that the full phrase, psalms and hymns and spiritual
songs, as it is used by Paul, is surely comprehensive and not
restrictive. It includes all lawful songs used in worship as
determined by the whole of Scripture. If the Holy Spirit
speaking through the inspired Apostle had meant to teach the
use of the Psalms exclusively, it would have been easy to have
said, 'teaching and admonishing one another *en biblo psalmon*
(with the book of Psalms)' as in Luke 20:42 and Acts 1:20,
leaving out entirely any mention of hymns and spiritual
songs."[196]

The fact that these Greek words, *psalmois*, *hymnois*, and
odais ("song" or "ode"), appear in Psalm titles in the Septuagint,
does not prove that they are technical terms for categories of
Psalms and refer to the Psalms exclusively. The fact is that the
Septuagint does not limit its use of *psalmois*, *hymnois*, and *odais*
to the book of Psalms. Habakkuk's psalm is called an "ode"

(Habakkuk 3:1, 19); and so it is with the "songs" of Moses (Exodus 15:1, Deuteronomy 31:19, 21, 22, 30; 32:44); Deborah's "song" (Judges 5:12); David's "song" (2 Samuel 22:1); and Solomon's "song" (1 Kings 4:32). Isaiah 42:10 uses the Greek word, *hymnon*, and commands us to sing unto the Lord a new song (or "hymn"). (Cf. Amos 5:23.) In Revelation 5:9 and 14:3, the new song of God's people is the Greek word for "ode," mentioned above, as is Moses' song in Revelation 15:3.

So then, "if the Word of God ought to be the standard and content for our worship and if the Psalms are the hymn book of the Bible, then it follows that the Psalms ought to be the standard and content of our singing. This is not the same as saying that we must sing Psalms exclusively."[197]

The Meaning of Hymns and Spiritual Songs

It is interesting to note that John Calvin, who "formulated this regulative principle with clarity and applied it with great consistency in the Reformation in Geneva . . . led his churches in the singing of metrical Psalms as well as various hymns: the metrical Decalogue [the Ten Commandments] followed by the 'Kyrie eleison' (Lord, have mercy) after each law, the Lord's Prayer in a long paraphrase, the Apostles' Creed sung, and the 'Nunc Dimittis (Luke 2:29–32) in meter."[198]

Calvin also is helpful in understanding the distinctions between psalms, hymns, and spiritual songs. "They . . . are commonly distinguished in this way—that a psalm is that, in the singing of which some musical instrument besides the tongue is made use of; a hymn is properly a song of praise, whether it be sung simply with the voice or otherwise; while the ode contains not merely praises, but exhortations and other matters. He (Paul) would have the songs of Christians, however, to be spiritual, not made up of frivolities and worthless trifles."[199]

William Hendriksen, a reformed commentator on the New Testament, also explains the distinctions between our three words: "The term psalms in all probability has reference, at least mainly, to the Old Testament Psalter; hymns, mainly to New Testament songs of praise to God and to Christ . . . and finally, spiritual songs, mainly to sacred lyrics dwelling on themes other than direct praise to God and Christ. There may, however, be some overlapping in the meaning of these three terms as used here by Paul."[200]

Some claim that the word, spiritual, meaning "Spirit-produced," modifies all three nouns, and that because they are "Spirit-produced" they are therefore Spirit-inspired psalms, hymns, and songs. However, this cannot be the case, since the Greek word for spiritual has a feminine ending, modifying songs, which is also feminine, while psalms and hymns are masculine, requiring masculine adjectives.

Assuming that the word, spiritual, means "Spirit-produced," and not simply "not made up of frivolities and worthless trifles," as Calvin thought, it should be observed that the biblical Psalms are *not* the only Spirit-produced songs in that sense. There are the songs of Moses (Exodus 15:1–18, Deuteronomy 32:1–43); the song of Miriam (Exodus 15:21); the song of Deborah (Judges 5:2–31); the song of David (2 Samuel 22:1–51, 1 Chronicles 16:8–36); the song of Habakkuk (Habakkuk 3:1–19); the Magnificat of Mary (Luke 1:46–55); the Benedictus of Zechariah (Luke 1:67–79); the song of the heavenly host (Luke 2:14); the Nunc Dimittus by Simeon (Luke 2:29–32); the song of John the Apostle (Revelation 1:5–7); and the songs of the saints (Revelation 4:8, 11; 5:9–10, 12–13; 7:10, 12, 15–17; 11:15–18; 12:10–12; 15:3–4; 16:5–7; 19:1–80). And we cannot forget the Song of Solomon, which is an entire book of the Bible. The book of Lamentations has a collection of five "psalms". The prophecies of Isaiah are filled with songs. Paul included probable hymns of the apostolic church in his epistles (Romans 11:33–36, Philippians 2:6–11, 1 Timothy 3:16). "It is difficult to believe that God would include so many songs in the Bible and not intend for them to be sung!"[201]

The Character of Singing in the Christian Church According to Ephesians 5:18–21 and Colossians 3:14–17

(Ephesians 5:18) The Power for Praise: The Filling of the Holy Spirit

(Ephesians 5:19) The Harmony of Praise: Singing to One Another

(Ephesians 5:19) The Content of Praise: Psalms, Hymns, Songs

(Ephesians 5:19) The Origin of Praise: The Heart

(Ephesians 5:19) The Focus of Praise: The Lord

(Ephesians 5:20) The Motive for Praise: Thanksgiving

(Ephesians 5:21) The Context of Praise: Mutual Submission in the Lord

(Colossians 3:14–16) The Presuppositions of Praise

(3:14) Love, the Perfect Bond of Unity

(3:15) Christ's Peace Ruling in the Hearts of Christians

(3:15) Gratitude

(3:16) Christ's Word Dwelling Richly in Christians

(Colossians 3:16) The Character of Praise

     With Wisdom

     Teaching and Admonishing One Another

     With Thanksgiving in Our Hearts to God

(Colossians 3:17) The Basis of Praise: The Name of Jesus Christ

The Musical Compositions of King Hezekiah for Public Worship

In Isaiah 38:20, we learn that King Hezekiah composed songs to be sung in the public worship of the people of God at the Temple: "so we will play my songs on stringed instruments all the days of our life at the house of the Lord." The Davidic Psalter had been in use for centuries in Israel, and King Hezekiah composed additional songs to be sung in worship.

The "Song Books" of the People of God in the Old Testament

The Psalter of the Bible was formed gradually over centuries by a variety of different authors, all inspired of the Holy Spirit (2 Timothy 3:16). It is divided into five books:

Book One contains Psalms 1–41

Book Two contains Psalms 42–72

Book Three contains Psalms 73–89

Book Four contains Psalms 90–106

Book Five contains Psalms 107–150

King David wrote most of the psalms (1000 B.C.), and Spirit-inspired authors added others until the time of the Babylonian Captivity (586–516 B.C.), as in Psalm 137, and the return of the Jewish people to Jerusalem in 500 B.C. Authors of the psalms include Solomon, Asaph, the sons of Korah, and Hezekiah. Psalms 46 and 48 are songs celebrating the defeat of Sennacherib and the deliverance of Jerusalem during the reign of Hezekiah. Jeremiah may have written psalm 71. And some of the Psalms are renditions of songs of praise from the days of Moses. (Compare Exodus 15 and Psalm 114).

Prior to the publication of the first edition of the Psalter, Israel had a songbook entitled, The Book of the Wars of the

LORD (Numbers 21:14), which was comprised of songs that celebrated Jehovah's blessings and Israel's victories in Him. The songs recorded in Numbers 21:14–15 and 21:17–18 are from that songbook. It was full of expressions of Israel's zeal and expectancy as she began to get the taste of victory. Songs from still other sources were used by the people of God in the praise of God such as the beautiful "Song of Deborah" in Judges 5:1.

The Development of a
Rich Psalmody-Hymnody in the Church

As Old Testament history of the covenant proceeded and divine revelation unfolded, the people of God would express the reality of covenant-redemptive-revelation and their experience of it in grateful songs of praise. Apparently it was King David's practice, (because of a probable custom in Israel), to versify the laws of God so that he and the people of God might learn them by heart and sing them in praise to God. God's Laws were sung along with the Psalms: "Your statutes are my songs in the house of my pilgrimage" (Psalm 119:54).

Another whole book of the Old Testament that was to be sung was the Song of Solomon. Furthermore, the prophets sometimes sang their prophecies: "Behold, you are to them like a sensual song by one who has a beautiful voice and plays well on an instrument; for they hear your words, but they do not practice them" (Ezekiel 33:32).

The Westminster Standards
and the Singing of Praise

The *Westminster Confession of Faith*, in its enumeration of the "parts of ordinary religious worship of God," lists "the singing of psalms" (21:5). Some have assumed that this statement supports exclusive psalmody. We must not accept this assumption too quickly. Although the wording is "the singing of the psalms," it is *not* "the singing of Psalms," nor "the singing of *the* Psalms." "Given their [the Westminster divines] tendency to over-capitalize (e.g., Atheism, Baptism,

Godhead, Idolatry, etc), it makes their choice of the small letter "p" in "psalms" all the more significant. Presbyterians are not bound by the divines' practice but by the wording of the Confession."[202] They appear to be using the word "psalms" in the sense of "any sacred song . . . sung in religious worship" (*Oxford English Dictionary*).

An able defender of exclusive psalmody[203] has sought to refute this interpretation of the Confession's use of *psalms* by arguing that: (1) "The authors of the Westminster Standards only capitalized the word Psalms when it was used as a *title* of the whole book;" (2) the Minutes of the Westminster Assembly prove that the divines held to exclusive psalmody; and (3) the *Westminster Directory for the Publick Worship of God* does not capitalize psalms when it is obviously referring to specific psalms in the book of Psalms. These appear to be formidable arguments. How can they be answered?

First, the assertion that the Westminster divines only capitalized the word "psalms" when giving the title of the whole book of Psalms is incorrect. Time and again they capitalized "psalms" when referring to individual Psalms throughout their Scriptural footnotes.

Second, whereas the minutes of the Westminster Assembly do clearly show that the divines wanted the church to sing the 150 psalms of the Bible in public worship, the minutes referred to do *not* indicate that they held to exclusive psalmody. They did believe that it was "useful and profitable to the Church that they be permitted to be publicly sung," but no argument in the minutes appears either for or against exclusive psalmody. The debates in the Assembly were with reference to which translations of the Psalms should be sung in worship.

Third, his argument that the *Westminster Directory for the Publick Worship of God* uses the uncapitalized word "psalm" or "psalms" specifically to indicate psalms in the biblical book of Psalms, on the other hand, is a credible one. It also says: "That the whole congregation may join therein, every one that can read is to have a psalm book; and all others, not disabled by age or otherwise, are to be exhorted to learn to read." But, once again, although the Westminster divines believed strongly in psalm-singing, these quotations cannot be used to prove more than that. They do not demand exclusive psalmody. It has not been proven whether or not all the Westminster divines held to exclusive psalmody.

Fourth, *The Westminster Confession of Faith* (21:5) sets forth the commanded parts of worship: The reading of the Scriptures with godly fear; the sound preaching, and conscionable hearing of the word, in obedience unto God, with understanding, faith, and reverence; singing of psalms with grace in the heart; as also the due administration and worthy receiving of the sacraments instituted for Christ; are all parts of the ordinary religious worship of God: besides religious oaths and vows, solemn fastings, and thanksgivings upon special occasions, which are, in their several times and seasons, to be used in a holy and religious manner. The relevant paragraph in the Confession was not meant to be exclusive or exhaustive in listing the elements of worship for the following reasons: First, it does not include the element of prayer, although prayer, of course, is explained in a previous paragraph. Second, the *Westminster Directory for the Publick Worship of God* also includes as elements of worship, the receiving of offerings and the pronouncing of the benediction.

CHAPTER ELEVEN

THE PLACE OF SPECIAL MUSIC IN THE WORSHIP OF GOD

Choirs of trained and paid singers had an important role in the tabernacle/temple worship of the covenant people of God in the Old Testament. Their elaborate arrangements were impressive and beautiful. 1 Chronicles 23:5 tells us that at one point the sanctuary choir and orchestra numbered four thousand people! First Chronicles 15:16 says, "Then David spoke to the chiefs of the Levites to appoint their relatives the singers, with instruments of music, harps, lyres, loud-sounding cymbals, to raise sounds of joy." Years later, when Solomon had finished building the temple, the priests and congregation assembled before the Ark of the Covenant, and the choir began the musical service: "All these were under the direction of their father to sing in the house of the LORD, with cymbals, harps and lyres, for the service of the house of God. Their number who were trained in singing to the Lord, with all their relatives, all who were skillful, was 288" (1 Chronicles 25:6–7). At the dedication of the temple, the Levitical singers "clothed in white linen, with cymbals, harps and lyres, standing east of the altar, and with them one hundred and twenty priests blowing trumpets in unison when the trumpeters and the singers were to make themselves heard with one voice to praise and glorify the LORD, and when they lifted up their voice accompanied by the trumpets and cymbals and instruments of music, and when they praised the LORD saying, 'He indeed is good for His lovingkindness is everlasting,' then the house, the house of the LORD, was filled with a cloud, so that the priests could not stand to minister because of the cloud, for the glory of the LORD filled the house of God" (2 Chronicles 5:12–14). In Solomon's temple, the sanctuary choir was a distinct body, furnished with homes and salaries (Ezekiel 40:44). The choir numbered two thousand singers and was divided into two choirs, who sang the Psalms antiphonally.

THE USE OF CHOIRS IN WORSHIP NOT CEREMONIAL

"Some argue that as such, choirs were merely part of the Temple ceremony. Therefore, when the purpose for the Temple had been fulfilled, the use of choirs passed away as well. Those opposed to choirs argue that choirs were part of the Old Testament ceremonial law. If that is the case, then, according to the Westminster Confession of Faith, 19:3, the New Testament has abrogated them. However, this assertion cannot stand up to examination, because it begs the question, 'In what way are choirs merely ceremonial?' This is a significant question, because choirs and musical instruments are not inherently ceremonial. They were not instituted at the time ceremonial worship was instituted with the Tabernacle, but about 500 years later. Hence, it must be demonstrated that choirs and instruments are inherently ceremonial in character and cannot be anything else. The reason that the ceremonial law has been abrogated is that it has been fulfilled in Christ. But what is there about choirs that point to Christ?"[204]

THE PURPOSE OF CHOIRS IN PUBLIC WORSHIP

The purpose of choirs and orchestras in worship, according to the Bible, is to raise sounds of joy, i.e., "to heighten the sound, both of the song and of the instrumental music, to the expression of festive joy in the Lord and His works."[205]

In fulfilling this divine purpose, choirs serve a dual role in the worship of God. First, they lead the congregation in singing. Second, they present special music to God on behalf of the congregation. Their role is to present music to God *on behalf of* the congregation, not *to* the congregation. "The anthem, or special music, provided by the choir or soloists is the functional equivalent of the pastoral prayer. It is an offering of prayer or praise to God (depending on the lyrical content) on behalf of the congregation. As such, it is an act of worship in its own right, and ought, like the pastoral prayer, to be done separately from any other part of the service, so that the congregation may fully join in."[206]

THE PLACE OF SOLOS IN PUBLIC WORSHIP

Several Scriptural texts reveal that solos were performed in the worship of God.

> I will give You thanks in the great congregation, I will praise You among a mighty throng. (Psalm 35:18)

The psalmist uses the first person singular pronoun with a singular verb, indicating that the congregation is not taking part. The Hebrew preposition, *be-*, meaning "in" or "among," confirms this view, because it indicates that the congregation is not necessarily included in the praise.

> He is not ashamed to call them brethren, saying, "I will proclaim Your name to My brethren, in the midst of the congregation I will sing Your praise." (Hebrews 2:11–12, which is a quote from Psalm 22:22)

In the Septuagint the Greek words for "in the midst of" is *en meso*, meaning "in the middle of," not *sun*, meaning "together with." The point is that "the one singing praise unto God is the same as the one declaring God's name to the brethren. No mention is made of any other individual being involved in either the preaching or the singing."[207] (Psalm 22 is messianic, and the speaker is ultimately Christ, but it also refers to the experience of the human author of the psalm.)

Women also apparently sang solos in the worship of God. In 2 Chronicles 35:25, Ezra 2:65, Nehemiah 7:67, Psalm 35:18, 111:1, the first person singular pronoun and singular verbs are equally appropriate for either a male or female. Women are specifically said to sing God's praises in Zephaniah 3:14, 2:10, Exodus 15:20–21, Judges 5:1, 1 Samuel 2:1, Luke 1:46, and 1 Chronicles 25:5–6.

In other words, if the congregation has gifted singers, their gifts should be used in the worship of God.

CHAPTER TWELVE

WHAT ABOUT DANCING
DURING WORSHIP?

More and more churches today are including in their public worship services choreographed dances and spontaneous dancing. Does this please God? Has God commanded that dancing be performed in the worship services of the Christian church today?

Dancing was a form of rejoicing in Old Testament Israel. Miriam and other women danced for joy with tambourines, singing God's praises for the Exodus redemption (Exodus 15:20). The Israelites danced around the golden calf at Sinai (Exodus 32:19). Jephthah's daughter greeted him with joy expressed in dancing with tambourines (Judges 11:34). The Benjaminites were given a plan to "catch" wives for themselves from the daughters of Shiloah by taking those women who take part in the dances (Judges 21:21, 23).

When David returned from killing Goliath, women from all the cities of Israel came out to greet him singing and dancing with tambourines and other musical instruments (1 Samuel 18:6). David defeated the unsuspecting Amalekites as they were eating, drinking, and dancing (1 Samuel 30:16). As the ark of the covenant was brought to Jerusalem, King David was dancing and leaping for joy before the Lord with all his might with the sound of musical instruments (2 Samuel 6:14, 16; 1 Chronicles 15:28-29. It should be noted that, although dancing was an important aspect of Hebrew culture, the Old Testament contains no instances of dancing in the actual tabernacle/temple worship services. We read of dancing prior to the Ark of the Covenant being placed in the tabernacle, but we read nothing of the dancing continuing during the worship service itself so it is therefore prohibited.

King Solomon, in the book of Ecclesiastes, says that there is a time to mourn and a time to dance (3:4). The prophet Isaiah described Babylon desolated by divine judgment as a place where shaggy goats frolicked and danced about (13:21). The prophet Jeremiah prophesied that under the New Covenant God would turn the mourning of His covenant people into joy, that He would rebuild them into greatness and holiness. He prophesied that under the New Covenant in Christ, His virgin people would take the tambourine and go forth to the dances of the merrymakers in great joy (31:4, 13). And in Lamentations 5:15, Jeremiah laments over Israel's apostasy saying that the joy of our hearts has ceased; our dancing has been turning into mourning.

When we come into the New Testament, we find fewer references to dancing. Matthew and Mark recount Salome's sensual dancing that led to the beheading of John the Baptist (14:6; 6:22). In Jesus' parable of the Prodigal Son, when the prodigal returned, music and dancing could be heard in the Father's house (Luke 15:25). And Jesus says that the men of his generation are like children who sit in the market place and call to one another; and they say, "We played the flute for you, and you did not dance; we sang a dirge, and you did not weep" (Luke 7:32).

In Psalm 30:11-12, we read, "You have turned for me my mourning into dancing; You have loosed my sackcloth and girded me with gladness; that my soul may sing praise to You, and not be silent." In two psalms God commands His people to praise him with dancing. In Psalm 149:3, God says, "Let them praise His name with dancing; Let them sing praises to Him with timbrel and lyre." And in Psalm 150:4, He says, "Praise Him with timbrel and dancing; Praise Him with stringed instruments and pipe."

In summary, dancing as a social amusement is rarely mentioned in the Bible, except in a general way, with one exception, Salome. "The other biblical references to dancing can be grouped unto two heads: the dance of public rejoicing, and the dance which was more or less an act of worship. The distinctly religious dance is more frequently mentioned. About the methods of dancing practiced by the ancient Hebrews but little is known. Probably the dancers in some cases joined hands and formed a ring, or part of a ring, as in some heathen representations. The description of David's dance: he danced before the Lord with all his might . . . leaping and dancing before the Lord, II Samuel 6:14-16, suggest three features of that particular display and the mode of dancing which it represented: violent exertion, leaping and whirling around. Perhaps the whirling dance of Islam is a modern parallel to the last. Women seem generally to have danced by themselves, one often leading the rest, both in dancing and antiphonal song. There seems to be some proof that the religious dance lingered among the Jews until the time of Christ and later."[208]

Now the question is: how are we to interpret these commands correctly, so that when we obey them in our worship of God we are neither adding to or subtracting from what God has commanded us?

To answer that question we must have a clear understanding of the hermeneutics of the Psalms, i.e., the correct interpretative principles for understanding the Psalms. The book of Psalms was written as poetry.[209] Therefore, it must be interpreted in terms of the distinctives of Hebrew poetry, which are basically three: strong imagery, hyperbole, and the use of parallelisms. Imagery is a verbal picture by means of metaphors, similes, and other figures of speech. Hyperbole is exaggeration for the sake of emphasis. Parallelism describes the heart of Hebrew poetry: usually two sentences of approximately the same length corresponding to each other in some way. The relationship between the two sentences is basic to understanding the parallelism.

With reference to our subject of dancing, we must understand the metaphors, images, and symbolism of the ancient Hebrews, without reading back into them our modern interpretations. "Our understanding of the meaning of the ancient biblical image comes about through, in the first place, imagining ourselves to be hearing the psalm for the first time when it was originally composed. We need to learn . . . for instance, what were the customs of shepherds in the ancient Near East...Thus it is important to first of all realize that the imagery of the Psalter is foreign to us. Second, we must ask how the first readers of the psalm would have understood the imagery."[210]

We should also remember that because Hebrew poetry is full of metaphors and imagery, it must not be interpreted with a wooden literalism. For example, when the Psalm says that God shall hide us under His feathers, this does not mean that God has wings! Therefore, any commands or exhortations in the Psalms must be interpreted according to the poetic *genre* of the Psalm, and not as we would interpret Mosaic legislation or historical narrative, for example. This means that when Psalm 150 commands us to praise God with "trumpet sound...harp and lyre...timbrel... stringed instruments and pipe...loud cymbals...(and) resounding cymbals," we should not interpret it literally as if we must praise God only with the musical instruments mentioned here and no others, regardless of our culture or time in history. Rather, we are to praise God in worship with every suitable instrument made available to us. And when the title of a specific Psalm tell us that the Psalm should be sung with the accompaniment of stringed instruments as Psalm 4, or with the flute as Psalm 5, or on the Gittith as Psalm 8, or set to Alamoth as Psalm 46, does that mean God is displeased when we sing them to the accompaniment of any other instrument?[211] Of course not. The point of these titles is to encourage us to have tunes and accompaniment that fit the theme and tone of the Psalm we are singing.[212]

Furthermore, recognizing the parallelisms of the poetry of the Psalms is a great help for interpreting the Psalms accurately. For example, the parallelism of Psalm 30:11 is full of metaphors:

> You have turned for me my mourning into dancing;
> You have loosed my sackcloth and girded me with gladness.

Throughout this psalm David is praising God for His help in enabling him to escape from his enemies so that he will spend the rest of his life praising Him. In the words of verse 11, David tells us that, while he was being persecuted, although he trusted in the Lord, he still experienced heaviness of heart and great sorrow. This sorrow was of "a godly kind" (2 Corinthians 7:10), for it moved David to repentance, and to testify to his repentance, he clothed himself in sackcloth. It was the practice of ancient Israel, when mourning, to dress in rough and unattractive sackcloth, made of the hair of animals, often with ashes placed on the head, to testify in these clothes of penitence, the intensity of their grief and/or conviction of sin.

By the grace of God, and through faith in Him, God delivered David, not only from his persecutors, but also from his grief and heaviness of heart. He changed his mourning into gladness. But we should notice the unforgettable way our parallelism says it. David says that God "turned his mourning into dancing by loosening his sackcloth and dressing him with gladness." What a picture! God himself took off David's clothes of grief and heaviness, reassured him of His favor, and clothed him with new clothes of joy and gladness; and in so doing transformed David's life of mourning into a life of dancing. The dancing parallels the "girded me with gladness," and the mourning parallels the "loosed my sackcloth." Did God literally do these things to David? Of course he did not. God did not literally take off one set of clothes and dress David in another. Even the phrase mourning into dancing is not a literal one. And yet God did really do in David's heart what these phrases pictured Him as doing. In reassuring Him of His favor, God removed David's heaviness of heart and replaced it with joy and gratitude. Therefore, we see in Psalm 30:11 how God takes customs of the ancient Israelites and uses them to reveal truths both they and we can understand and experience.

We no longer wear sackcloth when we are grieving, nor do we dance whenever we are happy; but we know very well the point that God is making here. We, as believers in Jesus, have experienced this psalm in our own Christian lives.

How does this help us interpret the commands of God in Psalm 149:3 and 150:4, to praise God with the timbrel, or tambourine, and dancing? Must these commands be taken in a literalistic sense in order to be taken seriously? In other words, is God commanding the Church that until the end of time, in every culture and era, we are to praise Him in worship by dancing with tambourines, and all the other instruments in Psalm 150, but with no other? Our answer is, "no!"[213] Why? These poetic commands are "bigger" and "richer" than that. To interpret the poetry of Psalms literally is to miss their main point. Every word of every Psalm must be taken truly, but not taken literally. The imagery, hyperbole and parallelisms of this poetry must be taken into consideration. And we must be able to see through the Hebrew cultural customs and practices to the message of each Psalm. "God did not speak to His people in a cultural vacuum. He spoke in terms that they understood. Since the Psalms originated in an ancient, oriental society, the imagery arises from that culture. Thus, much of the imagery is foreign to modern, Western experience. Our understanding of the meaning of an ancient biblical image comes about through, in the first place, imagining ourselves to be hearing the psalm for the first time when it was originally composed. Thus it is important to first of all realize that the imagery of the Psalter is foreign to us. Second, we must ask how the first readers of the psalm would have understood the imagery."[214]

The Hebrew custom was to wear sackcloth when showing sorrow, but that does not mean that we today must wear sackcloth in prayer when we feel under conviction of sin. Rather we should feel the intensity of the conviction of sin and be moved by it to repentance. The Hebrew custom was to rejoice with an energetic kind of dancing, involving leaping and whirling, with tambourines and other musical instruments, often lead by women. Does that mean that we today must learn how they danced in their ancient culture and learn how to play the musical instruments they played, if our worship is to be pleasing to God? No. But our praises of the Lord should be exuberant, public, joyous, and full of understanding and emotion.

> "At that time," declares the Lord, "I will be the God of all
> the families of Israel, and they shall be My people. . . .
> "Again I will build you, and you will be rebuilt,
> O virgin of Israel!
> Again you will take up your tambourines,
> And go forth to the dances of the merrymakers.
> Again you will plaint vineyards
> On the hills of Samaria . . . "
> For the Lord has ransomed Jacob,
> And redeemed him from the hand of him who
> was stronger than he.
> "They will come and shout for joy on the height of Zion,
> And they shall be radiant over the bounty of the Lord—
> Over the grain, and the new wine, and the oil,
> And over the young of their flock and the herd;
> And their life shall be like a watered garden,
> And they will never languish again.
> Then the virgin shall rejoice in the dance,
> And the young men and the old, together;
> For I will turn their mourning into joy." (Jeremiah 31:1–13)

Here we see the power and beauty of imagery. Jeremiah 31 is messianic prophecy. Most specifically, it is a prophecy of the blessings and promises and effects of the New Covenant in Jesus Christ (Hebrews 8:8f, 10:16f). God will return to His people in Jesus Christ (30:23–31:1), and all of life will be renewed for them, from worship to agriculture (31:2–6). God will regather and rebuild his church from Jews and Gentiles (31:8–10), in a "new exodus." By the sacrifice of Christ, God will redeem, or ransom, his people from their sins (31:11); and in Christ, he will pour out abundant bounty on His people (31:12–14). In the future, from Jeremiah's perspective, God's people would be characterized, not by apostasy, but by gratitude and praise to God for the joyous experience of His abundant bounty to them in Christ. Their rich and full lives under God's blessing would be like a watered garden. The totality of their days would be spent in the celebration of the goodness and grace of God shown them in Christ. God will turn their mourning into gladness and their grief into joy. He will satisfy them with fat things – fullness of life and prosperity.

In prophesying these things, Jeremiah used idiom and imagery that Israel of his day understood, for his prophecy was not only for our benefit. By his preaching he was endeavoring to lead the people to repentance by reminding them what they used to be, what they are during his days, and what they will be someday in Christ. Therefore, although every word of this prophecy of the New Covenant and its blessings has come true or will come true in Christ and His Church, nevertheless that does not mean that every word is to be interpreted literally. Why? Because the New Testament does not interpret all of these prophecies literally. For example, according to Jeremiah, the New Covenant in Christ is made with the house of Israel and the house of Judah (31:31), but the New Testament applies it to the Church, comprised of both Jews and Gentiles (Hebrews 8:8f; 10:16f; 12:22f).

Furthermore, we must not miss all the imagery in Jeremiah 31. The new Israel is spoken of as a virgin (v. 4). The new Israel, the visible catholic church of Christ, will rejoice in Christ. The text should not be interpreted that throughout history in every area of the globe where the church exists, Christians will be dancing—whirling and leaping in near eastern fashion—with tambourines. If we interpret this passage literalistic, and not as poetry, which it is, then we must believe that this prophecy of the New Covenant is fulfilled only when virgins are dancing with tambourines, with young and old men (v. 13), and Christians are planting vineyards on the hills of

Samaria (v. 5), when watchmen on the hills of Ephraim shall call out, "Arise, and let us go up to Zion . . . " (v. 6). And, more importantly, the text, if literally interpreted, applies the blessings of the New Covenant only to ethnic Israel, i.e., the remnant of Israel (v. 7), not to the visible catholic church. It is on this kind of allegedly literal interpretation of Old Testament prophecies that dispensational pre-millennialism has been built. However, to interpret these poetic prophecies literally, written in the idiom and imagery of ancient Israel, forces an unbiblical hermeneutic upon the Word of God. The literary form of each text determines the way we interpret the text.

So then, are we subtracting from the regulative principle of worship by not dancing before the Lord in our public worship services? If our above interpretations are correct, the answer is "no."

CHAPTER THIRTEEN

WHAT DOES THE BIBLE SAY ABOUT HAND CLAPPING?

More and more churches today include hand clapping in public worship. Does this please the Lord? Does the Lord require it today? One thing for sure is that applause in the praise of man, either musicians or speakers, is totally out of place in the worship of God, for He said: "I am the LORD, that is My name; I will not give My glory to another" (Isaiah 42:8). But does applause have any other purpose in worship? We often hear charismatic preachers exhorting their congregations to "give the Lord a big hand." Is this what God intended when He inspired the psalmist to write Psalm 47?

> O clap your hands, all peoples;
> Shout to God with the voice of joy.
> For the Lord Most High is to be feared,
> A great King over all the earth.[215] (Psalm 47:1–2)

We should remember, as we learned in our previous discussion on "Dancing before the Lord," that since the Psalms are poetry, they must be interpreted as poetry and not as historical narrative in a literalistic fashion. We must take into consideration the imagery, hyperbole, and parallelisms that distinguish Hebrew poetry.

Throughout the Psalms, the imagery is beautiful, dramatic, and often intense. Consider Psalm 113:5–6.

Who is like the Lord our God,
Who is enthroned on high,
Who humbles Himself to behold
The things that are in heaven and in the earth?

Here God is pictured, metaphorically, as seated on a magnificent throne that is so high above us that from it one can see our whole planet and even the entire universe. This is an awesome picture of the sovereignty of God. Is God sitting on a literal throne stooping down to see the earth? Of course not!

Why do the psalmists use so much imagery? Although imagery is less precise than literal language, it is not less accurate. To say "the enemy is ruthless and cruel," is more precise than to say "the enemy is a lion," but both are accurate. But why not be precise all the time? Why bother with images? When using images, whatever is lost in precision is gained in vividness of expression. Further, the images, as in poetry in general, speak to us more fully than regular literal language. They stir our emotions, attract our attention, and also stimulate our imaginations, as well as help us discover some new truth about the objects compared.

We can illustrate all of these points with another example. At the end of Psalm 78 we find the following simile:

Then the Lord awoke from His sleep,
As a man wakes from the stupor of wine.
He beat back His enemies;
He put them to everlasting shame. (vv. 65–66)

"This image gets our attention immediately! The comparison is between the Lord and a man arising after a deep sleep. What is more, almost shockingly, the man's sleep is deep as the result of consuming too much wine. Now that the image has grabbed our attention, what do we discover from it? The psalm as a whole concerns the rebellious history of Israel . . . As a result of their rebelliousness, God . . . wasn't present with them . . . The last few verses (vv. 65–72) describe how God made His presence dwell with Israel again during David's time. It was as if God was sleeping and now had awakened to help His people. The picture is vivid and striking and communicates its point well and in a way that can't fully be paraphrased in literal language. This is because images speak not only to our minds but to our hearts as well."[216]

Another thing should be remembered about biblical imagery. "God did not speak to His people in a cultural vacuum. He spoke in terms that they understood. Since the Psalms originated in an ancient, oriental society, the imagery arises from that culture. Thus, much of the imagery is foreign to modern, Western experience. Our understanding of the meaning of an ancient biblical image comes about through, in the first place, imagining ourselves to be hearing the psalm for the first time when it was originally composed. Thus it is important to first of all realize that the imagery of the Psalter is foreign to us. Second, we must ask how the first readers of the psalm would have understood the imagery."[217]

How are we to take the command of God to the world's nations in Psalm 47:1 to clap their hands and shout the Lord's praises? Psalm 47 is a song of triumph probably in celebration of the victory of King Jehoshaphat over the Ammonites and Edomites recorded in 2 Chronicles 20. All the nations (KJV) or peoples (NASV) of the world, the entire Gentile world, are summoned publicly and energetically to rejoice that Jehovah is their rightful Sovereign and the mighty Victor over all His enemies, by a mighty applause and loud shouting for joy.

Again, the question is how are we to interpret this command? Does it mean that if the church today is not including literal hand clapping and loud shouting in its worship service, it is disobeying the Lord's command and therefore violating the regulative principle of worship by subtraction? The command that the world's nations shout for joy and applaud the Lord for His mighty works makes no mention that this is to be done in the worship services of the tabernacle or temple. We have no record in the Bible of worshippers shouting or clapping their hands in tabernacle/temple worship services.

In Israel the clapping of hands was a common gesture displaying joy, triumph, and applause (Nahum 3:19, Psalm 98:8, Isaiah 55:12). Israelites would also give audible expression to joy and exuberance by shouting or singing loudly for joy. In Psalm 47:5 we read that:

God has ascended with a shout (or amid shouting),
The Lord, with (or amid) the sound of a trumpet.

Here God is pictured as returning to heaven after the conquest of His enemies and the deliverance of His people, as in Psalm 7:8. The shouting and the sound of the trumpet are from those in heaven welcoming God's return with public and joyous praise celebrating His triumph. Therefore, as the citizens of heaven joyous and publicly praise God for His victory, so the church on earth is publicly, energetically and joyously to sing His praises. Did the immense, infinite, and omnipotent God literally ascend from earth to heaven? No.[218] Was He welcomed with shouting and trumpets when He "returned" to heaven? No. It is all a metaphor. The psalmist is using customs familiar to Israel to impress the people of God with the triumph of Almighty God, to whom the shields of the earth belong (47:9). Does God literally have the shields of His defeated enemies lining the halls of His palace? No. But the message is a clear and powerful one.

The meadows are clothed with flocks,
And the valleys are covered with grain;
They shout for joy, yes, they sing. (Psalm 65:13)

When God visits the earth (65:9), to manifest His abundant generosity, kindness, and loving care for it, the whole creation rejoices in shouts and songs of praise. Are meadows literally clothed with flocks of sheep? No. Do the meadows and valleys shout for joy and sing? No. But the point cannot be missed. God attributes well-known customs of the ancient Hebrews to creation and His point is vividly and beautifully made.

Break forth and sing for joy and sing praises.
Let the sea roar and all it contains,
The world and those who dwell in it.
Let the rivers clap their hands;
Let the mountains sing together for joy
Before the Lord; for He is coming to judge the earth.
(Psalm 98: 4, 7–9)

Once again all created things are commanded by God to sing God's praises. The sea and everything in is to break forth singing for joy. All the rivers of the world are to clap their hands. All the mountain ranges are to sing together for joy, because the Lord is coming to judge the earth, to remove all the effects and consequences of sin from His creation. Is God commanded the rivers literally to clap their hands? Of course not! Will the mountains literally sing for joy? No. But the point is powerfully made.

So will My word be which goes forth from My mouth;
It will not return to Me empty,

Without accomplishing what I desire,
And without succeeding in the matter for which I sent it.
For you will go out with joy,
And be led forth with peace;
The mountains and the hills will break forth into shouts of joy before you,
And all the trees of the field will clap their hands.
(Isaiah 55:11–12)

Not only will individual believers and their families experience the joy and peace of salvation by the Word of God, but all of creation will feel the transforming effects of that powerful Word, and the response of creation will be universal praise for the Creator: "the trees of the field will clap their hands." Literally? No. But Israel knew what Jehovah meant by these words.

Psalm 47, as all the Psalms, is full of beautiful and moving imagery. The nations are to clap their hands and shout God's praise, but nations do not have hands to clap or mouths with which to shout. God does not literally subdue nations under our feet (v. 3). The omnipresent God does not ascend (v. 5). Heaven was not literally filled with shouts and the sound of the trumpet when God "returned" from helping Jehoshaphat defeat the Ammonites and Edomites (v. 5). An infinite and omnipresent God neither "ascends" nor "returns." God does not literally sit on a throne (v. 8). The "shields of the earth" also is obviously a metaphorical phrase (v. 9). And the rivers and trees do not literally clap their hands, but they do manifest the glory of their Maker and Redeemer.

We even use the word, "applause," (the clapping of the hands), figuratively, as well as literally. We would say to someone who has done a noble deed, "We applaud you," without necessarily implying that we want everyone present to clap his hands. We "shout" the Lord's praises, as we sing His praises exuberantly and energetically, to the best of our ability, and publicly in congregational worship.

Therefore, we are not disobeying God and violating the regulative principle of worship by not including literal applause and loud shouting in our public worship services. God is not commanding us in the West today to adopt the customs of an ancient people in the Near East if we are to worship God properly. Rather, we are commanded, in Old Testament idiom and metaphor, to celebrate the victories of our Sovereign God and Redeemer, intensely, publicly, joyfully, and energetically with intelligence and emotion.

CHAPTER FOURTEEN

WILLIAM CUNNINGHAM ON THE AUTHORITY OF APOSTOLIC EXAMPLE

The following is taken from William Cunningham's book, *Historical Theology*.[219]

"There can be no reasonable doubt that it may be justly laid down as a general principle, that apostolic practice, such as that exemplified in the Council at Jerusalem [Acts 15], does impose a permanent binding obligation in regard to the constitution and government [and worship] of the church, and the administration of its affairs . . . The truth of this general principle seems very clearly deducible from these two positions—first, that Christ commissioned and authorized the apostles to organize His church as a distinct visible society, and to make provision for preserving or perpetuating it to the end of the world; and secondly, that the apostles, in executing this branch of their commission, have left us few direct or formal precepts or instructions as to the constitution and government [and worship] of the church, and have merely furnished us with some materials for ascertaining what it was that they themselves ordinarily *did* in establishing and organizing churches, or what was the actual state and condition of the church and the churches while under their guidance . . . but as they were executing their Master's commission when they were establishing and organizing churches . . . and as there is no intimation in Scripture, either in the way of general principle or of specific statement, that any change was ever after to take place in the constitution and government of the church, or that any authority was to exist warranted to introduce innovations, the conclusion from all these considerations, taken in combination, seems unavoidable, that the practice of the apostles, or what they actual did in establishing and organizing churches is, and was intended to be, a binding rule to the church in all ages; that the Christian churches of subsequent times ought, *de jure*, to be fashioned after the model of the churches planted and superintended by the apostles...One very obvious limitation of it is, that the apostolic practice which is adduced as binding, must be itself established from the Word of God, and must not rest merely upon materials derived from any other and inferior source. This position is virtually included in the great doctrine of the sufficiency and perfection of the written Word...a doctrine held by Protestants in opposition to the Church of Rome. If this doctrine be true, then it follows that anything which is imposed upon the church as binding by God's authority...must be traced to, and established by, something contained in, or fairly deducible from, Scripture" (pp. 64–65).

"[However] everything which the apostles did or sanctioned, connected with the administration of the affairs of the church, is not necessarily and *ipso facto*, even when contained in and deduced from Scripture, binding universally and permanently upon the church. It has, for instance, been the opinion of the great body of divines of all sects and parties, that the decrees of the Council of Jerusalem [Acts 15], simply as such, and irrespective of anything else found in Scripture bearing upon any of the subjects to which they refer, were not intended to be of universal and permanent obligation, and are not now, in fact, binding upon Christians. It was undoubtedly made imperative upon the churches of that age by the decree of the Council, to abstain from things strangled, and from blood; but the great body of divines of all parties have been of opinion, that an obligation to abstain from these things was not thereby imposed permanently upon the church, and is not now binding upon Christians...There were some things which, from their nature, seem to have been local and temporary, suited only to the particular circumstances of the church in that age, and in the countries where the gospel was first preached; and these have been generally regarded as destitute of all permanent binding force" (pp. 66–67).

"[Any doubt or uncertainty] as to *some* of the applications of the principle affords no ground for the use which some have made of it in rejecting the principle altogether, and denying that apostolic practice, ordinarily and as a general rule, forms a binding law for the regulation of the affairs of the church. The general considerations already adverted to establish the truth of the general position as to the ordinary binding force of apostolic practice" (p. 67).

[The following are some general rules of Cunningham to guide us in determining which practices of the apostles are binding upon the church:]

1. "Nothing ought to be admitted into the ordinary government and worship of the Christian church which has not the sanction or warrant of Scriptural authority, or apostolic practice at least, if not precept...[other than the "circumstances concerning the worship of God" exception]...

2. "The Scriptural proof of any arrangement or practice having existed in the apostolic churches ordinarily and *prima facie* imposes an obligation upon all churches to adopt it...

3. "The [burden of proof] lies upon those who propose to *omit* anything which has the sanction of apostolic practice, and that they must produce a satisfactory reason for doing so, derived either from some general principle or specific statement of Scripture bearing upon the point..." (p. 68).

APPENDIX A

James Bannerman on the Limits of Church Authority in Worship Services

The following quotes are taken from James Bannerman's book, *The Church of Christ.*[220] (Bannerman was a leading Scottish theologian of the 19th Century whose books are still available from modern publishers.)

The power of the Church in reference to worship is limited in four ways: by a regard to its *source*, or the authority of Christ; by a regard to its *rule*, or the Word of God; by regard to its *objects*, or the liberties and edification of the members of the church; and by a regard to its own *nature*, as exclusively spiritual. We shall find that in each of these ways the power of the Church in regard to the worship of God is restricted; and that the exercise of it in imposing human rites and ceremonies, as part of that worship, is condemned" (p. 363).

I. The exercise of Church power in reference to the worship of God is limited by a regard to the source of that power, or the authority of Christ. If the Lord Jesus Christ be the only source of authority within His own Church, then it is abundantly obvious that it is an unlawful interference with that authority for any party, civil or ecclesiastical, to intermeddle with His arrangements, to claim the right to regulate His institutions, or to pretend to the power of adding to, or of taking away from, or altering His appointments" (p. 363).

In the province of Divine worship as much as in the province of Divine truth, He claims the sole right to dictate and impose His appointments on men...He claims as His exclusive right, authority to dictate what observances and institutions of worship He sees best for the approach of sinners to God in a Church state; and it is a usurpation of His power for the Church itself to assume a right to regulate His institutions, to add to His appointments, and superinduce its own provision for worship upon His" (pp. 364–65).

II. The exercise of Church power in the matter of worship is limited by a regard to its rule, or the revealed Word of God... There can be no law for the regulation of Divine service, any more than for any other department of the Church's duty, except the law of Scripture, to the exclusion of the arbitrary will or capricious discretion of all parties, civil or ecclesiastical...In the department of worship as well as in the department of doctrine, the Church has no latitude beyond the express warrant of Scripture, and is forbidden as much to administer a worship not there revealed, as to preach a Gospel not there revealed. The single fact that the rule of Church power in the worship of God is the rule of Scripture, is decisive of the whole controversy in regard to rites and ceremonies, and ties up the Church to the ministerial office of administering a directory made for it, instead of presumptuously attempting to make a new directory for itself" (p. 367).

There is no possibility of evading this argument, except by denying that the Scriptures are the only rule for worship, or by denying that they are a sufficient one. Neither of these denials can be reasonably made. The Scriptures are the only rule for worship, as truly as they are the only rule for the Church in any other department of her duties. And the Scriptures are sufficient for that purpose; for they contain a directory for worship, either expressly inculcated, or justly to be inferred from its statements, sufficient for the guidance of the Church in every necessary part of worship. There are, *first*, express precepts contained in Scripture, and designed to regulate the practice of Divine worship in the Church as to ordinances and services; *second*, there are particular examples of worship in its various parts recorded in Scripture, and both fitted and intended to be binding and guiding models for subsequent ages. And, *third*, when neither express precepts nor express examples are to be met with, there are general Scripture principles applicable to public worship, enough to constitute a sufficient directory in the matter. Anything beyond that directory in the celebration of worship is unwarranted and superstitious. And the danger of tampering with uncommanded rites and observances is not small. Let the evil of 'teaching for doctrines or duties the commandments and ordinances of men' be once introduced into the Church, and a departure from the simplicity of Scripture worship once begun, and superstitions will strengthen and grow apace" (p. 368).

III. The exercise of Church power in the worship of God is limited by a regard to its objects, or to the liberties and edification of the members of the Church. The introduction of human rites and ceremonies into the worship of the Church, by ecclesiastical authority, very directly goes to oppress the consciences and abridge the spiritual freedom of Christ's people. In so far as the provisions of public worship are appointed by Christ, and expressly regulated in His Word, the plea of conscience cannot lawfully come in to resist their observance, or object against the enforcement of them. Conscience has no right, and can possess no liberties, in opposition to the ordinances of Him who is the Lord of the conscience. But the rights of conscience furnish a plea that may lawfully be urged in opposition to ordinances and ceremonies imposed by mere human authority, and enforced by ecclesiastical power. In so far as the provisions of worship in the Church are merely human, and not of Christ, the conscience of the members who are called upon to comply with such provisions, when grieved and offended, has a right to be heard and respected" (p. 370).

Every part of Church worship, because an ordinance of God, is binding upon the conscience by authority: it imposes a kind of obligation which no other solemnity can impose. And when, as part of that ordinance, there is introduced some rite or ceremony or appointment of man, claiming to have an equal authority, and to lay upon the conscience the same obligation, however harmless it may be in itself, it is an offence against the liberty and rights of the Christian people of the Church...To lay down a formula of Church worship of her own, to appoint rites and ceremonies of her own, and to enforce these under the alternative of forfeiture of Church fellowship, is a violent and unlawful encroachment upon the conscience and the liberties of Christ's people" (pp. 370–71)

IV. The exercise of Church power in the worship of God is limited by the proper nature of that power, as exclusively spiritual. There are no more than *two* ways in which a properly spiritual power can be brought to bear upon the souls of the worshippers in public worship. There may be, in the first place, a spiritual power or virtue connected with the truth which the Church publishes, by which it produces a spiritual effect on the soul. Or there may be, in the second place, a sacramental grace or virtue connected with the outward and sensible ordinances which the Church administers, by which they produce a spiritual effect on the soul. In the one case, it is the Spirit of God employing the teaching of truth by the Church as the channel through which He communicates a spiritual virtue. In the other case, it is the Spirit of God employing the dispensation of ordinances by the Church as the channel through which He communicates a spiritual virtue...But beyond these means of spiritual grace, the Spirit of God does not usually go. He does not employ the inventions and ordinances of men as His instruments in either of these two ways" (pp. 372–73).

The Spirit of God does not employ the rites and ceremonies of men to be teaching signs in the Church, and to communicate truth; nor does He make these rites and ceremonies, as mystical or significant types declaring the truth, to be a spiritual power in the hearts of men" (p. 373).

The Spirit of God does not employ human rites and ceremonies in the second way I have mentioned, or as ordinances linked with spiritual grace, instead of or in addition to those of Divine appointment...As human and not Divine ordinances, the Spirit of God does not employ them as means of grace; nor does He pour through the channel of their administration by the Church the tide of His spiritual influence. They are of man, and not of God; and therefore they carry with them no spiritual blessing from the Spirit" (pp. 374–75)

The only power which the Church is the instrument of dispensing through ordinances is the power of the Spirit, given not to human inventions, nor in connection with ecclesiastical and uncommanded ceremonies, but only to the ordinances and Sacraments appointed by God" (p. 375).

Notes

Introduction

[1] Some of the critics of the regulative principle of worship, an emphasis taught in several sections of the *Westminster Confession of Faith and Catechisms* (I,VI; XX, II; XXI, I; XVI, I; LCQ. 3; LCQ. 108; LCQ 109; SCQ. 2), have taken a vow to God regarding those Westminster Standards which says: "Do you sincerely receive and adopt the Confession of Faith and the Catechisms of this Church, as containing the system of doctrine taught in the Holy Scripture?"

[2] Among those in the Reformed camp who have rejected the Westminster Confession's regulative principle of worship, it is common also to hear the rejection of the Confession's statements on the nature of baptism, the requirements for taking the Lord's Supper, the office of preaching, the nature of Presbyterian church government, the nature of the covenant, the nature of justification, and more. What will be next?

[3] See James Jordan, *Liturgical Nestorianism* (Niceville, FL: Transfiguration Press, 1994). John Frame's terminology reveals the influence of this article on his thinking.

Chapter One

[4] John Frame uses Numbers 16:46 in an effort to show that Nadab and Abihu did not add to the commands of God, rather they transgressed God's command to take their fire from the fire on the altar. Their fire was "strange" in that it was taken from some private source. However, Numbers 16:46 "simply says that fire is to be taken from the altar and put on a censer. Neither in this or any other passage are people expressly told not to use fire from any other source. The point of the regulative principle is that when God says, 'Take fire from the altar,' men must follow God's direction without adding their own human rules or traditions. The passage that Frame offers as proof, Exodus 35:3, that fire from another source is expressly

forbidden teaches that the people are not to kindle a fire in their dwellings on the Sabbath. It has nothing to do with the Leviticus 10:1 passage" (Brian Schwertley, *Sola Scriptura and the Regulative Principle of Worship*, [http://www.reformed.com/pub/sola_b.htm], Appendix B, footnote #196). I will be quoting and paraphrasing Brian Schwertley's refutations of the arguments of the critics of the regulative principle of worship because he ably defends, exegetically and theologically, the regulative principle, and also because he refutes its critics in greater detail than any one I have read. The three articles written by Schwertley from which I will draw are: 1) *A Brief Critique of Steven M. Schlissel's Articles Against The Regulative Principle of Worship* (http://www.all-of-grace.org/pub/schwertley/schlissel.html); 2) "The Neo-Presbyterian Challenge to Confessional Presbyterian Orthodoxy: A biblical Analysis of John Frame's *Worship in Spirit and in Truth*" (http://www.reformed.com/pub/sola_b.htm); and 3) *Sola Scriptura and the Regulative Principle of Worship* (http://www.reformed.com/pub/sola.htm).

[5] Schlissel, in his usual manner, mocks those who say that the issue was "strange fire" not "strange incense," as he supposes. He writes: "Well now, we find ourselves here entering the arena of Clintonian rhetoric . . . It was a package deal. 'Strange fire' clearly encompasses the incense which it was burning. To parse these as regulativists try to do is like saying, 'It depends on what the word "is" is'" ("All I Really Need to Know About Worship . . . I Don't Learn from the Regulative Principle," 1:8, endnote 2). However, if our text means "strange incense" why did it not say "strange incense," since "strange incense" is expressly forbidden in Exodus 30:9? Why does Schlissel want to change the wording to something it does not say? (Where is first?) Second, "package deal" or not, Nadab and Abihu were guilty of offering "strange fire." And third, "the fact that they were consumed by fire certainly favors the interpretation that their sin was strange fire and not strange incense" (Schwertley, *A Brief Critique*).

[6] Samuel Kellogg, *The Book of Leviticus* (Minneapolis, Minnesota: Klock and Klock Christian Publishers, 1978 reprint), 239.

[7] Quoted by Philip Martin in *The Biblical Doctrine of Worship: A Symposium* (Pittsburgh, PA: Crown and Covenant Publishing Co., 1974), 27.

[8] Schwertley, *A Brief Critique.*

[9] Nineteenth century Bible commentator, George Bush, argues vigorously that this phrase, "which He did not command them," is a figure of speech called meiosis. This figure is a rhetorical understatement, a kind of hyperbole, which represents a thing less than it is. Therefore Bush concludes that our phrase is "probably equivalent to saying, 'which the Lord had pointedly forbidden.'" However, such exegesis reveals Bush's assumptions regarding worship, which color his interpretation. Doing things in worship that God has not commanded is in no way an understatement, nor is it hyperbole. To say that this phrase represents the actions of Nadab and Abihu as less sinful than they were is to fail to appreciate the evil of adding to the Word of God and seeking to worship Him in ways He has not commanded.

[10] Schwertley, *A Brief Critique.*

[11] Martin, *The Biblical Doctrine of Worship*, 9.

[12] John L. Girardeau, "The Discretionary Power of the Church," *Sermons* (Columbia, S.C.: The State Company, 1907), 397.

[13] John Calvin, *Commentaries on Four Last Books of Moses*, vol. III (Grand Rapids, Michigan: William B. Eerdmans Publishing Company, 1979 reprint), 431.

[14] Martin, *The Biblical Doctrine of Worship*, 29.

[15] See Gary North's discussion of this point in his *Sanctions and Dominion: An Economic Commentary on Numbers* (Tyler, Texas: Institute for Christian Economics, 1997), 175-181.

[16] Jeremiah 19:5 makes essentially the same point: "Because they . . . have built the high places of Baal to burn their sons in the fire as burnt offerings to Baal, a thing which I never commanded or spoke of, nor did it ever enter My mind" (vv. 4-5).

[17] Martin, *The Biblical Doctrine of Worship*, 313.

[18] Schwertley, *A Brief Critique*.

[19] "Howsoever manifold wickedness might have been challenged in that which they did, yet if any would dispute with God upon the matter, He stoppeth their mouths with this one answer, I commanded it not, neither came it into My heart" (George Gillespie, quoted in Martin, *The Biblical Doctrine of Worship*, 313).

[20] John Calvin, *Commentary on the Prophet Jeremiah*, vol. IX, 413-414.

[21] Deuteronomy 12:32: "Whatever I command you, you shall be careful to do; you shall not add to nor take away from it."

[22] Steve Schlissel argues that the regulative principle of Deuteronomy 12:32 was applied only to the sacrificial system of worship connected with the tabernacle. Since Christ did away with the whole ceremonial system by His death and resurrection, the regulative principle of Deuteronomy 12:32 no longer applies so that there is no regulative principle at all in the New Covenant. One of the problems with Schlissel's position, and we will deal with others later, is that the Bible contains several passages that apply the regulative principle beyond the ceremonial worship of the tabernacle. And as Brian Schwertley has written, "If even one passage can be shown to apply the regulative principle outside of tabernacle/temple worship, then Schlissel's whole argument is worthless" (Schwertley, *A Brief Critique*, 13). Four such passages are Mark 7:1, Matthew 15:13, Colossians 2:20-23, and John 4:22.

[23] "The arguments offered by Schlissel (and others such as Doug Wilson) regarding the regulative principle are not new but are (in general matters) restatements of old prelatical arguments long ago rejected by the Reformed churches. Note the words of Zacharias Ursinus (written in the 1570s and first published in the 1580s): 'There are some who object to what we have here said, and affirm in support of will-worship, that those passages which we have cited as condemning it, speak only in reference to the ceremonies instituted by Moses, and of the unlawful commandments of men, such as constitute no part of the worship of God, and not of those precepts which have

been sanctioned by the church and bishops, and which command nothing contrary to the Word of God. But that this argument is false, may be proven by certain declarations connected with those passages of Scripture to which we have referred, which likewise reject those human laws, which, upon their own authority, prescribe anything in reference to divine worship which God has not commanded, although the thing itself is neither sinful nor forbidden by God. So Christ rejects the tradition which the Jews had in regard to washing their hands, because they associated with it the idea of divine worship, although it was not sinful in itself, saying, "Not that which goeth into the mouth defileth a man, but that which cometh out of the mouth, this defileth a man. Woe unto you Scribes and Pharisees, hypocrites; for ye make clean the outside of the cup and platter, but within ye are full of extortion and excess" (Matt. 15:11, 23, 25). The same thing may be said of celibacy and of the distinction of meats and days, of which he calls doctrines of devils although in themselves they are lawful to the godly, as he in other places teaches. Wherefore, those things are also which are in themselves indifferent, that is neither commanded nor prohibited by God, if they are prescribed and done as the worship of God, or if it is supposed that God is honored by our performing them, and dishonored by neglecting them, it is plainly manifest that the Scriptures in these and similar places condemn them'" (Schwertley, *A Brief Critique*).

[24] See chapter 8: "James Bannerman on the Limits of the Church Authority in Worship," 127f.

[25] Schwertley, *Sola Scriptura*, chapter 5, section 3.

[26] James Bannerman, *The Church of Christ*, vol. I (Edmonton, AB Canada: Still Waters Revival Books, 1991), 337.

[27] Schwertley, *A Brief Critique*.

[28] John Owen, "A Discourse on Liturgies," *Works*, XIX (London: Richard Baynes, 1826 reprint), 398.

[29] Schwertley, *Sola Scripture*, "Summary and Conclusion" (footnote #127).

[30] Michael Bushell, *The Songs of Zion* (Pittsburgh, PA: Crown and Covenant Publications, 1993), 120.

[31] Although many of the most able defenders of the Reformed regulative principle of worship also subscribe to exclusive psalmody and non-instrumental music in the worship of God, I am not convinced by their arguments and exegesis. I see their views as contradictions to the regulative principle of worship, for the Bible does command both to be done in congregational worship.

[32] Schwertley, *A Brief Critique.*

[33] *Ibid.*

[34] James H. Thornwell, *The Collected Writings of James Henley Thornwell*, vol. I (Edinburgh, Scotland: The Banner of Truth Trust, 1974 reprint), 173.

[35] Robert L. Dabney, *Lectures in Systematic Theology* (Grand Rapids, Michigan: Zondervan Publishing House, 1975 reprint), 363.

[36] Martin, *The Biblical Doctrine of Worship*, 118.

[37] R.C.H. Lenski, *Interpretation of St. John's Gospel* (Minneapolis, Minnesota: Augsburg Publishing House, 1943), 325.

[38] Bushell, *The Songs of Zion*, 149, 151-152.

[39] *Martin*, The Biblical Doctrine of Worship, *118.*

[40] Colossians 3:20-23 also disproves the argument that the regulative principle of worship of Deuteronomy 12:32 applied only to the tabernacle/temple of the Old Testament and was abrogated when Christ came and fulfilled tabernacle/temple worship in Himself and His ministry. "The apostle Paul, writing under the inspiration of the Holy Spirit several years after the regulative principle was supposedly abolished, rigorously enforced the regulative principle. Paul says that any addition to what God has commanded or authorized is self-imposed religion . . . Paul says that adding to God's Word is a show of false humility. Can man improve upon the worship and service that God has instituted?" (Schwertley, *Sola Scriptura*, chapter 5, section 3.2).

[41] By means of this metaphor in 2:16, Paul is saying that "the heretical teachers [are] assuming to themselves the position of arbiters and disqualifying the Colossian believers for failing to keep their ritualistic [and ascetic] rules" (Herbert Carson, *The*

Epistles of Paul to the Colossians and Philemon, Tyndale New Testament Commentaries [Grand Rapids, Michigan: Wm. B. Eerdmans Publishing Co, 1972], 73).

[42] On the implications of Paul's condemnation of Jewish ceremonialism referred to in Colossians 2:16, see: "Did Paul Do Away with the Fourth Commandment?" on page 147.

[43] This does not mean that immature and unknowledgeable people, such as children, can disobey the civil government, the church, or the parent, with a high hand, as if the understanding of the immature and unknowledgeable were infallible. Such an attitude is only an excuse and cover for rebellion, rooted in human pride. Humility is required toward superiors.

[44] Bannerman, *The Church of Christ*, Vol. I, 369-371.

[45] Owen, "A Discourse on Liturgies," *Works*, XIX, 460.

[46] John Eadie, *A Commentary on the Epistle of Paul to the Colossians* (Grand Rapids, Michigan: Zondervan Publishing House, 1957 reprint), 199-200.

[47] Carson, *The Epistles of Paul to the Colossians and Philemon*, 7.

[48] Hendriksen, *Exposition of Colossians and Philemon*, New Testament Commentary (Grand Rapids, Michigan: Baker Book House, 1973), 131.

[49] Bannerman, *The Church of Christ*, vol. I, 375.

[50] Thomas Watson, *A Body of Divinity* (Grand Rapids, Michigan: Sovereign Grave Publishers, reprint), 267.

[51] Schwertley, *Sola Scriptura*, chapter 5, section 3.2.

[52] Calvin, *Commentaries*, vol. XXI, 181.

[53] This is Schwertley's word in *Sola Scriptura*, chapter 5, section 3.2.

[54] *Ibid.*

[55] McCracken, *The Biblical Doctrine of Worship*, 79.

[56] John Calvin, *Sermons on Deuteronomy* (Edinburgh, Scotland: The Banner of Truth Trust, 1987 reprint), 113–114.

[57] McCracken, *Biblical Doctrine of Worship*, 80.

[58] John L. Girardeau, "The Discretionary Power of the Church," *Sermons*, 378.

CHAPTER TWO

[59] Calvin, *Sermons on Deuteronomy*, 113.

[60] Young, *The Biblical Doctrine of Worship*, 310.

[61] Bannerman, *The Church Of Christ*, vol. I, 343f.

[62] Thomas Ridgeley, *Commentary on the Larger Catechism*, vol. II (Edmonton, Canada: Still Waters Revival Books, 1993 reprint), 330.

[63] Quoted by Schwertley, *Sola Scriptura*, chapter 5, section 1.

[64] Schwertley, *Sola Scriptura*, chapter 5, section 1.

[65] *Ibid.*

[66] *Ibid.*

[67] *Ibid.*, chapter 5, section 3.

[68] *Ibid.*

[69] *Ibid.*

[70] *Ibid.*

[71] *Ibid.*

[72] Bushell, *The Songs of Zion*, 71-72, quoted in *Sola Scriptura*, chapter 5, section 3.

[73] Schwertley, *Sola Scriptura*, chapter 5, section 3.

[74] John Owen, "A Discourse on Liturgies," *Works*, XIX, 444.

[75] Young, *The Biblical Doctrine of Worship*, 307.

[76] "There is of course careful distinction to be made between the Word of God and inferences drawn from the Word of God. We may challenge the validity of inferences drawn from Scripture and attempt to determine whether they are indeed scriptural, but we may never in the same way challenge the validity of the explicit statements of Scripture. The words and statements of Scripture are absolutely authoritative. Their authority is underived and indisputable. The authority of valid inferences from Scripture, on the other hand, is derivative in nature, but one cannot argue that such inferences are therefore less authoritative than the express declarations of Scripture. They simply make explicit what is already expressed implicitly in Scripture" (Bushell, *The Songs of Zion*, 124).

[77] Robert Shaw, *The Reformed Faith* (Inverness, Scotland: Christian Focus Publications, 1974 reprint), 16.

[78] John Girardeau, *The Discretionary Power of the Church* (http://www.reformed.org/documents/dogma/disc_power.html), par. 20.

[79] Quoted by Schwertley in "The Neo-Presbyterian Challenge to Confessional Presbyterian Orthodoxy: A Biblical Analysis of John Frame's *Worship in Spirit and in Truth*" (http://www.reformed.com/pub/sola_b.htm).

[80] Robert Shaw, *The Reformed Faith*,16.

[81] Quoted by Schwertley, *Sola Scriptura*, chapter 5, section 7.

[82] Bannerman, *The Church of Christ*, vol. I, 349.

[83] Girardeau, *The Discretionary Power of the Church*, par. 28.

[84] *Ibid.*, par. 34.

[85] Bannerman, *The Church of Christ*, vol. I, 351.

[86] *Ibid.*, 352.

[87] *Ibid.*, 352f.

[88] This book was originally printed in 1641 and reprinted in 1993 by Naphtali Press, P.O. Box 141084, Dallas, Texas, 75214.

[89] Bannerman, *The Church of Christ*, vol. 1.

[90] George Gillespie, *English Popish Ceremonies* (Dallas, TX: Naphtali Press, 1993 reprint), 281.

[91] *Ibid.*, 283f.

[92] *Ibid.*, 284.

[93] Bannerman, *The Church of Christ*, vol. 1, p. 357.

[94] *Ibid.*, 358.

[95] Girardeau, *The Discretionary Power of the Church*, par. 35-36.

[96] Schwertley, *Sola Scriptura*, chapter 5, section 4.3.

[97] John Frame, *Worship in Spirit and in Truth* (Phillipsburg, NJ: Presbyterian and Reformed Publishing Co., 1996), 40-41.

[98] Schwertley, *A Brief Critique*.

[99] James H. Thornwell, *Collected Writings*, vol. II, 163, quoted in Schwertley, *A Brief Critique*.

[100] Girardeau, *The Discretionary Power of the Church*, par. 46.

CHAPTER THREE

[101] Gary North, *The Sinai Strategy: Economics and the Ten Commandments* (Tyler, Texas: Institute for Christian Economics, 1986), 26.

[102] John Calvin, *John Calvin's Sermons on the Ten Commandments* (Grand Rapids, Michigan: Baker Book House, 1980), 67.

[103] Wilhelmus à Brakel, *The Christian's Reasonable Service*, vol. III (Morgan, PA: Soli Deo Gloria Publications, 1992 reprint), 105.

[104] Calvin, *Sermons on the Ten Commandments*, p. 66.

[105] Two things should be remembered about the Law of God in the Bible. (1) It is all-inclusive (Jude 22–23). Under a particular sin forbidden or duty commanded *all causes, means, occasions, appearances, and provocations* are included. (2) The Law of God is two-sided (Eph. 4:28). Where a specific duty is commanded of us, the opposite sin is implicitly forbidden; and where a specific sin is expressly forbidden, the opposite duty is implicitly demanded.

Chapter Four

[106] Owens, "A Discourse Concerning Liturgies," *Works*, XIX, 448-449.

[107] Girardeau, *The Discretionary Power of the Church*, par. 45.

[108] *Ibid.*, par. 46.

Chapter Five

[109] Schwertley, *The Neo-Presbyterian Challenge*.

[110] Calvin, *Sermons on Deuteronomy*, 284, 285, 286.

[111] For a refutation of the "Purim argument" against the regulative principle, see page 104f.

Chapter Six

[112] This argument is answered on pages 52f and 54.

[113] Schwertley, *Sola Scriptura*, chapter 5, section 2.

[114] Psalm 22:22, 25 – "I will tell of Your name to My brethren; in the midst of the assembly I will praise You . . . From You

comes my praise in the great assembly; I shall pay my vows before those who fear Him."

[115] Psalm 27:4 – "One thing I have asked from the Lord, that I shall seek: that I may dwell in the house of the Lord all the days of my life, to behold the beauty of the LORD, and to meditate in His temple."

[116] Psalm 84:1-2 – "How lovely is Your dwelling places, O Lord of hosts! My soul longed and even yearned for the courts of the Lord; my heart and my flesh sing for joy to the living God." John Calvin explains that in this verse, "David complains of his being deprived of liberty of access to the Church of God, there to make a profession of his faith, to improve in godliness, and to engage in divine worship . . . He knew that God had not in vain appointed the holy assemblies, and that the godly have need of such helps so long as they are sojourners in this world" (Quoted in Schwertley, *Sola Scriptura*, chapter 5, section 2).

[117] Psalm 87:2 – "The Lord loves the gates of Zion more than all the other dwellings of Jacob." David Clarkson concludes from this verse: "Public worship is to be preferred before private. So it is by the Lord, so it should be by His people" (Quoted in Schwertley, *Sola Scriptura*, chapter 5, section 2).

[118] Ecclesiastes 5:1-2 proves that public worship is unique and special. "Guard your steps as you go to the house of God and draw near to listen rather than to offer the sacrifice of fools; for they not know they are doing evil. Do not be hasty in word or impulsive in thought to bring up a matter in the presence of God. For God is in heaven, and you are on the earth; therefore let your words be few." As Matthew Henry points out: "When we are in the house of God, we are in a special manner before God and in his presence, there where he has promised to meet his people..." (Quoted in *Sola Scriptura*, chapter 5, section 2).

[119] Schwertley, *Sola Scriptura*, chapter 5, section 2.

[120] Shaw, *The Reformed Faith*, 227-228.

[121] This position is addressed on pages 17f, 52f, and 55f.

[122] See page 63f.

[123] See page 18f.

[124] Douglas Bannerman, *The Scripture Doctrine of The Church* (Grand Rapids, Michigan: Baker Book House, 1976 reprint), 134.

[125] Alfred Edersheim, *The Life And Times of Jesus The Messiah*, vol. I, (New York: Longmans, Green, and Co., 1910), 434.

[126] Quoted in Schwertley *A Brief Critique*.

[127] See pages 21, 31, and 48.

[128] See page 68.

[129] Schwertley, *A Brief Critique*.

[130] Matthew Henry, *A Commentary on the Whole Bible* (Peabody, Massachusetts: Hendrickson Publishers, 1992 reprint), 1:420.

[131] Matthew Poole, *A Commentary on the Holy Bible* (Peabody, Massachusetts: Hendrickson Publishers, 1985 reprint), 2:117–118.

[132] R.J. Rushdoony, *Institutes of Biblical Law* (Phillipsburg, NJ: The Craig Press, 1973), 763.

[133] Bannerman, *The Scripture Doctrine of the Church*, 134.

[134] *Ibid.*

[135] The sequence of liturgical elements in the synagogue was usually as follows: (1) prayers of thanksgiving or "blessings"; (2) the Confessing of the Shema, i.e., Deuteronomy 6:4-5; (3) prayer with the response of "Amen" from the congregation; (4) the reading of a passage from the Pentateuch; (5) the reading of a passage from the Prophets; (6) a sermon or word of exhortation usually with a Messianic reference; (7) The Benediction pronounced by a priest, if available, to which the congregation responded, "Amen."

[136] Schwertley, *A Brief Critique*.

[137] Alfred Edersheim, *The Life and Times of Jesus The Messiah*, vol. I, 431.

[138] Schwertley, *Sola Scriptura*.

[139] I have seen these things engraved on the walls of ancient synagogues, in such places as Capernaum and Chorazin. Furthermore, the services at the synagogues generally corresponded with the same days and hours as temple services. In the construction of synagogues, the desire was to conform to the temple arrangements as much as possible, as the ruins of ancient synagogues testify. The plan of a synagogue would

often be a general imitation of the plan of the temple. In some synagogues the holy lamp was never allowed to go out, imitating the undying light in the temple. The sacred scrolls of the Law and the Prophets were stored in the synagogues in a container called "the Ark." Generally, the middle of the synagogue was elevated, from which elevation the Law was read and expounded. If a Levitical priest was in attendance at synagogue worship, he would be asked to come forward and pronounce the benediction on the congregation, after which the congregation would respond, "Amen." The leader of worship in the synagogue would wear a jacket similar to that worn by the priests, although he himself was not a priest.

[140] Bushell, *The Songs of Zion*, 71-72.

[141] Schwertley, *The Neo-Presbyterian Challenge*.

[142] Alfred Edersheim, *History of the Jewish Nation After the Destruction of Jerusalem Under Titus*, 381, quoted by Schwertley, *Sola Scriptura*, chapter 5, section 5.

[143] Some use Matthew 26:23 to prove that Jesus participated in the religious hand washing of the Seder. However, we know that is not the case for two reasons: (1) The parallel text of John 13:26 explains Matthew 26:23, not as Jesus washing his hands by dipping them in a bowl of water, but Jesus dipping bread in a cup of wine. (2) "[I]f Jesus and the disciples celebrated the Seder as it is set forth in the Mishnah (as many assert) [with hand washing of religious and symbolic significance], then Christ was guilty of participating in the exact same ritual that earlier in the gospel accounts he and his disciples refused to do and which elicited a scathing condemnation of the Pharisees by our Lord. We regard such a scenario as exegetically and theologically impossible. There are other problems with the idea that Jesus followed the Seder according to Mishnah. For instance, the gospel accounts do not speak of four cups [of wine] but merely one which was shared by all the disciples" (Schwertley, *Sola Scriptura*, chapter 5, footnote #100).

[144] The "Seder theory" is based on the Jewish Mishnah, "a compilation of rabbinical oral traditions from 200 B.C. to A.D. 200," most of which were compiled around A.D. 189. As the respected Jewish Christian scholar, Alfred Edersheim, pointed

out: "'It has already been hinted more than once that the law laid down in the Mishnah frequently represents the theories and speculations of the Jewish doctors of the second century A.D., and not the actual practice of any given period. Several of their regulations deal accordingly with obsolete customs, and have little regard to the actual circumstances of the time'" (Edersheim, *History of the Jewish Nation after the Destruction of Jerusalem under Titus*, 381, quoted by Schwertley in *Sola Scriptura*, chapter 5, section 5).

[145] Schwertley, *Sola Scriptura*, chapter 5, section 5.

[146] George Gillespie, *English Popish Ceremonies*, 269-270.

[147] Schwertley, *Sola Scriptura*, chapter 5, section 5.

[148] Schwertley, *A Brief Critique*.

[149] *Ibid.*

[150] For observing occasional days of thanksgiving, see the *Westminster Directory for the Public Worship of God*, in the section entitled, "Concerning the Observation of Days of Public Thanksgiving."

[151] Schwertley, *Sola Scriptura*, chapter 5, section 6.

[152] M'Crie, *Lectures in the Book of Esther*, 298-300, quoted by Schwertley, *Sola Scriptura*, chapter 5, section 6.

[153] Finally, the argument based on a misrepresentation of the regulative principle is answered on page 59.

Chapter Seven

[154] Owen, *Works*, vol. XIX, 454.

[155] Thomas M'Crie, "On the English Liturgy," *The Miscellaneous Writings* (Edinburgh, Scotland: John Johnstone, 1841), 210.

[156] Bannerman, *The Church Of Christ*, vol. I, 383.

[157] John L. Girardeau answered this argument previously, on pages 72-76.

[158] Samuel Miller, *Presbyterianism: They Truly Primitive and Apostolical Constitution of the Church of Christ* (Philadelphia, PA: Presbyterian Board of Publication, 1835), 67-68.

[159] *Tracts Against Fisher, The Jesuit*, 377, quoted in Samuel Miller, *Presbyterianism*, 70.

[160] Miller, *Presbyterianism*, 70.

[161] Ibid., 71-72.

[162] *Ibid.*, 72.

[163] J. King Hewison, *The Covenanters*, vol. I (Glasgow, Scotland: John Smith and Son, 1913), 43.

[164] Professor Mitchell quoted in Hewison, *The Covenanters*, 43.

[165] *The Covenanters*, vol. I, 42-44.

[166] I have never understood the reason for ministers wearing their academic gowns and hoods with their three "doctor stripes" on the sleeves in the public worship of God, unless it is pride of intellect.

[167] Transubstantiation has been Roman Catholic doctrine since A.D. 1215. It teaches that in the Lord's Supper the bread is literally transmuted into Jesus' physical body, and the wine is literally transmuted into Jesus' blood, so that the recipient literally eats and drinks Jesus' physical flesh and blood.

[168] Miller, *Presbyterianism*, 86.

[169] *Ibid.*, 87.

[170] *Ibid.*, 82.

[171] *Ibid.*, 93.

Chapter Nine

[172] Quoted by James Hastings Nichols in *Corporate Worship in the Reformed Tradition* (Philadelphia, PA: The Westminster Press, 1968), 35.

[173] Quoted by Rodney N. Kirby in "Instrumental Music," an unpublished paper, Cherokee Presbyterian Church, Woodstock, GA.

[174] Kirby, "Instrumental Worship."

Chapter Ten

[175] Joseph Pipa, *The Lord's Day* (Inverness, Scotland: Christian Focus Publications, 1997), 101.

[176] *Ibid.*

[177] *Ibid.*

[178] *Ibid.*, 117.

[179] *Ibid.*, 120.

[180] John Murray, *The Epistle to the Romans*, *NICNT*, vol. II (Grand Rapids, Michigan, Wm. B. Eerdmans Publishing Co., 1964), 258.

[181] Robert L. Dabney, *Discussions: Evangelical and Theological*, vol. I (London: The Banner of Truth Trust, 1967 reprint), 496-550

[182] *Ibid.*, 496-550.

[183] *Ibid.*

[184] *Ibid.*

[185] Pipa, *The Lord's Day*, 128.

[186] *Dabney*, Discussions, *vol. I, 496-550.*

[187] Murray, *Romans*, *NICNT*, vol. II, 258-259.

[188] *Ibid.*, 259.

[189] For more information on the sinfulness and danger of celebrating uncommanded holy days, see page 112-113f.

CHAPTER ELEVEN

[190] The reason we are dealing with this subject is because some who believe the regulative principle of worship say that faithfulness to the regulative principle requires exclusive psalmody. My view is that exclusive psalmody requires unfaithfulness to the regulative principle.

[191] *The Harbinger*, edited by David Goodrum, Marietta, GA, published several helpful articles refuting exclusive psalmody: (1) "Thoughts on Psalmody," by Gary Crampton (July-August 1993). (This article was published in *The Counsel of Chalcedon* [May 1991] and in the *Trinity Review* [October 1992].) (2) "Instrumental Worship," by Rodney N. Kirby (September-October 1993); (3) "Exclusive Psalmody and Doing God's Will as it is Fulfilled in Christ," by Leonard Coppes (November-December 1993); (4) "What Should We Sing?", by Daniel R. Morse (January-February 1994); (5) "The Regulative Principle and Singing in Worship," by Stephen Pribble (January-February 1994); and (6) "A Defense of Special Music," by Stephen Pribble (January-February 1994).

[192] Leonard Coppes, "Exclusive Psalmody and Doing God's Will as it is Fulfilled in Christ," *The Harbinger* (November-December 1993).

[193] Exclusive psalmodists claim that since God has commanded us to sing only the 150 psalms of the Bible in worship, it is therefore sinful to sing anything else. If that is the case, since the word *Jesus* does not occur in the 150 psalms, it would be sinful to sing the word *Jesus* in the public worship of God. This fact makes this view intolerable to me.

[194] This word study of the Hebrew words for "psalm," "hymn," and "song" was done by Stephen Pribble in "The Regulative Principle and Singing in Worship," published by *The Harbinger* (January-February 1994): 13.

[195] *Ibid.*, 17.

[196] *Ibid.*, 18.

[197] Morse, "What Should We Sing?", 7.

[198] William D. Maxwell, "Calvin's French Rites at Strasbourg and Geneva," *A History of Christian Worship* (New York: Oxford University Press, 1936), 112-119.

[199] John Calvin, *Commentaries*, 3:16.

[200] William Hendriksen, *New Testament Commentary: Exposition of Ephesians*, (Grand Rapids, Michigan: Baker Book House, 1967), 240.

[201] Pribble, "The Regulative Principle and Singing in Worship," 20.

[202] *Ibid.*, 28 footnote.

[203] This able defender of exclusive psalmody is my good friend, Brian Schwertley, upon whom I have leaned so heavily in this book in his refutations of Schlissel, Frame, and Wilson. His arguments against Pribble's view of *psalms* in the Confession are found in his paper, *The Neo-Presbyterian Challenge*.

Chapter Twelve

[204] Benjamin Shaw, *Studies in Church Music* (Greenville, SC: Greenville Presbyterian Theological Seminary, 1993), 17.

[205] *Ibid.*, 18.

[206] *Ibid.*, 22.

[207] Pribble, "A Defense of Special Music," 5.

CHAPTER THIRTEEN

[208] James Orr, Gen. Ed., *The International Standard Bible Encyclopaedia*, vol. II (Grand Rapids, Michigan: Wm. B. Eerdmans Publishing Co., 1974 reprint), 1169f.

[209] Why were the Psalms written in poetry? "Poetry appeals more directly to the whole person than prose does. It stimulates our imaginations, arouses our emotions, feeds our intellects and addresses our wills. More than this, poetry is pleasurable. It is attractive to read and even more so to read aloud (or sing)" (Tremper Longman III, *How to Read the Psalms* [Downers Grove, IL: InterVarsity Press, 1988], 92).

[210] Longman, *How To Read The Psalms*, 118.

[211] The titles of various psalms, written by the author of the psalm they introduce, are inspired of the Holy Spirit. "The titles introducing individual psalms give information about the author, the historical occasion which prompted the writing, the melody, the psalm's function, and occasionally, other matters [such as musical accompaniment]" (*How to Read the Psalms*, 38).

[212] It is interesting to note that the NASV's marginal note regarding the meaning of "Shiggaion" in the title of Psalm 7 says that it is "a wild passionate song"!

[213] The timbrel "is here accompanied by its inseparable adjunct *dancing*, which might seem misplaced in a list of instruments, and those employed in sacred music, but for the peculiar usages and notions of the ancient Hebrews, with respect to this external sign of joy" (J.A. Alexander, *The Psalms Translated and Explained* [Grand Rapids, Michigan: Baker Book House, 1975 reprint], 564). "*The dance* was in early times one of the modes of expressing religious joy, Exodus 15:20, II Samuel 6:16. When from any cause men's ideas shall undergo such a revolution as to lead them to do the same thing for the same purpose, it will be time enough to discuss that matter. In our time, dancing has no such use, and cannot, therefore, in any wise by justified by pleading the practice of pious Jews of old" (William Plumer,

quoted by Charles Spurgeon, *The Treasury of David*, vol. VII, 441).

[214] Longman, *How to Read the Psalms*, 118.

CHAPTER FOURTEEN

[215] The Hebrew word for shout in Psalm 47:1, 5; Psalm 65:13; Psalm 132:16, etc., means "to express joy by shouting or singing energetically."

[216] Longman, *How to Read the Psalms*, 116-117.

[217] *Ibid.*, 118.

[218] Psalm 47:5 does have a messianic implication, in that it can be applied to the literal ascension of Jesus Christ. However, His ascension and exaltation were in His humanity.

[219] *William Cunningham, Historical Theology, vol. I (Edinburgh, Scotland: The Banner of Truth Trust, 1969 reprint), 64f.*

[220] *Bannerman,* The Church of Christ, *vol. I, 360.*